William Greenwell

**The Electrum Coinage of Cyzicus**

William Greenwell

**The Electrum Coinage of Cyzicus**

ISBN/EAN: 9783743345430

Manufactured in Europe, USA, Canada, Australia, Japa

Cover: Foto ©ninafisch / pixelio.de

Manufactured and distributed by brebook publishing software (www.brebook.com)

William Greenwell

**The Electrum Coinage of Cyzicus**

# THE ELECTRUM COINAGE

# OF CYZICUS

BY

WILLIAM GREENWELL, M.A., D.C.L.,

F.R.S., F.S.A.,

MEMBER OF THE NUMISMATIC SOCIETY OF LONDON.

*WITH SIX PLATES.*

LONDON:
ROLLIN AND FEUARDENT,
61, GREAT RUSSELL STREET, W.C.
AND
4, RUE DE LOUVOIS, PARIS.
1887.

# CONTENTS.

|  | PAGE |
|---|---|
| INTRODUCTION. | |
| Purpose of the essay | 1 |
| Previous accounts of staters | 2 |
| Position of Cyzicus | 3 |
| Oldest settlers there | 3 |
| Argonauts in connection with Cyzicus | 5 |
| Colonized from Miletus | 5 |
| Historical account of the state | 6 |
| Religious origin of coinage | 7 |
| Authentication of the currency | 8 |
| Divinities worshipped at Cyzicus: Cybele, Apollo, Artemis, Persephone, Dionysus | 9 |
| Importance of Cyzicus as a trading community | 12 |
| No early gold or silver currency there | 13 |
| Monetary standard, the Phocaic | 13 |
| Electrum, the metal used for the coinage of Cyzicus; its nature and composition | 14 |
| Electrum an artificial and not a natural alloy | 15 |
| Did it pass as current for gold? | 16 |
| Monetary value of the Cyzicene stater | 17 |
| Cyzicenes, the principal currency on the coasts of the Euxine Sea during the fifth century B.C. | 18 |
| Source of supply of gold for the coinage | 19 |
| First issue of staters, apparently a single one | 21 |
| Second issue, one of long continuance and variety | 22 |
| Name of the city not found on staters | 22 |
| Types on the coinage | 23 |
| Representations of gods on the staters | 23 |
| Other subjects, such as heroes, &c. | 26 |
| Coin subjects, sometimes adopted from the coins of other states | 27 |
| Large and varied number of types on the coinage | 29 |
| Magisterial devices and not the badge of the state, the principal subject on the staters | 30 |
| More than one type issued in the course of a year | 30 |
| Period of time during which the staters were issued | 31 |
| Principal issue commenced about B.C. 500 | 32 |
| Classification of staters in respect of date | 32 |
| Time when the staters ceased to be issued | 34 |
| Art at Cyzicus | 35 |
| Coinage not a complete index of artistic wealth | 36 |
| Skill of Cyzicene die-engravers | 37 |
| Shown in the power of adapting subject to space | 38 |
| Subjects derived from groups on friezes, &c. | 39 |
| Discoveries of staters as single coins or in hoards | 41 |

|  | PAGE |
|---|---|
| TABLE OF DENOMINATIONS | 43 |
| SEPARATE ACCOUNT OF EACH TYPE | 45 |
| Type of earliest stater | 45 |
| Types connected with gods, &c. | |
| Zeus | 46 |
| Poseidon | 48 |
| Demeter | 51 |
| Apollo | 55 |
| Artemis | 60 |
| Pallas | 60 |
| Gaia | 63 |
| Cecrops | 64 |
| Aphrodite | 65 |
| Hermes | 66 |
| Dionysus | 66 |
| Scylla | 73 |
| River God | 73 |
| Nike | 74 |
| Eleutheria | 76 |
| Cybele | 77 |
| Atys | 78 |
| Heracles | 82 |
| Odysseus | 86 |
| Orestes | 87 |
| Perseus | 88 |
| Warriors | 96 |
| Harpy | 100 |
| Sphinx | 101 |
| Lion | 102 |
| Chimæra | 108 |
| Bull | 109 |
| Horse | 110 |
| Ass | 112 |
| Ram | 112 |
| Goat | 113 |
| Boar | 114 |
| Dog | 115 |
| Griffin | 117 |
| Eagle | 119 |
| Fish | 121 |
| Prow | 124 |
| Helmet | 125 |
| Lyre | 125 |

# THE ELECTRUM COINAGE OF CYZICUS.

It is not my intention in this account of the electrum coinage of Cyzicus to enter upon a history of the state in any of its relations, except so far as it may afford an elucidation of my more immediate subject. The purpose of the essay is to bring together as complete a list as is possible of all the electrum coins issued by Cyzicus during the long period of their emission, together with a reproduction by the autotype process of each type. It is hoped that this in itself will be of service to numismatists and others interested in Hellenic art and its development.

No attempt to publish a full list of these numerous coins has hitherto been made since the time of Sestini, whose catalogue, on account of the scarcity of types then known, was necessarily a very imperfect one. I have long felt that until a detailed, and to a very large extent an exhaustive account was given, it was impossible that this most valuable and extensive series of coin-types could be presented to numismatic science with any prospect of being adequately studied. In the hope, therefore, that I may be able to supply these important materials for study and research to those desirous of becoming acquainted with the marvellous series of the Cyzicenes, I have prepared this account of them, the result of much labour, but not undertaken without quite corresponding pleasure. The work lays claim to be little more than an accurate catalogue, though I have also sought to make it useful to those not deeply acquainted with Hellenic mythology and its various cults, by some illustrative matter in connection with the different types.

Of this remarkable and large series of coins, Eckhel, as I shall have occasion to mention again, knew nothing. The first account of them was given by Sestini in his *Stateri antichi*, published in 1817, where figures of several staters and parts of the stater are given, not, however, very correctly. The next account is one by M. Charles Lenormant, *Essai sur les Statères de Cyzique*, in the first volume of the new series of the *Revue Numismatique*, in 1856, followed in 1864 by a paper by his son M. François Lenormant, *Statères inédits de Cyzique*, in the ninth volume of that periodical. The same learned author has also given an account of the coins of Cyzicus in *Dictionnaire des Antiquités* of Daremberg and Saglio. Though I am unable to agree with these eminent authors in some of their views, I feel myself under great obligations to them for much information and many suggestions. Two most valuable papers by Mr. B. V. Head have appeared in the *Numismatic Chronicle*, new series, vols. xvi. and xvii., "On a recent find of Staters of Cyzicus," and "Additional Notes," &c., the latter being accompanied by a letter from M. Six containing many valuable remarks on some of the staters described in Mr. Head's first paper. Several scattered notices of one or more of these coins have been given by De Koehne, Mr. Borrell, Dr. Imhoof-Blumer, and Herr Löbbecke in various serials.

It remains to mention Marquardt's very complete work, *Cyzicus und sein Gebiet*, published in 1836. Though a small space only is devoted to the electrum coinage—indeed at the time he wrote not many staters, &c., were known—on all other subjects connected with the state he gives a very full account, and I am indebted to him for much of the material I have used in this essay.

The pleasing task is left me of expressing my deep obligation to the keepers of the various public collections noticed in the following account of the different coins, and to the private collectors who have most freely placed their coins at my disposal for publication. To Mr. Poole and the other officers of the Medal Room in the British Museum it is impossible for me to fully express my gratitude, for the courteous and untiring way in which they have received me in my numerous visits to that splendid collection, and for most valuable information and counsel.

---

The position of Cyzicus was one admirably fitted for the site of a great trading community. It shows us how the genius of the Hellenic race instinctively selected places suitable for colonization, and which afforded scope for the development of that spirit of commercial enterprise, which, existing at the time of our earliest acquaintance with that people, has continued with many vicissitudes to our own day. The town was placed on the neck of a promontory which projected into the Propontis (Sea of Marmora), on the northern coast of Mysia, about the middle of the waterway between the Ægean and Euxine Seas, and had therefore the advantage not only of the local trade with the opposite coast of Thrace, but of the wider traffic with the various towns on the shores of the two important seas between which it was planted.

The oldest settlers in Cyzicus are stated to have been Doliones, who were seated on the skirts of the Mysian

Olympus and around the shores of Lake Ascanius. This people had probably relations with the Hellenic stock, but had affinity also with the Phrygians. They in this way became influenced by the religious culture and civilisation of the more eastern branches of the great Hellenic family, which extended itself through Thrace to Hellas proper and to countries still farther to the west. Mysians, we are told, were settled in the plain of the river Æsepus, a kindred people, differing little either in habits or language from the earlier occupants. To these were added Phrygians from Thrace, and the whole population became so intermixed and fused that neither the autochthons nor the later immigrants can be separated the one from the other. It is due, probably, to there not having been any very distinctive difference between the several elements of the population that the inhabitants became one, and to some extent a homogeneous people. The next occupation was by Pelasgi from Thessaly, driven out thence by the Æolians, and who at a still earlier period had been dispossessed of Magnesia by Cretheus, son of Æolus. According to Conon, the author of the Διηγήσεις, their leader was Cyzicus, son of Apollo, or, as was otherwise said, of Æneus and Ænete, daughter of a Thracian king, Eusorus. Cyzicus was married to Cleite, daughter of Merops, king of Percote; but according to another account he died unmarried, though about to take to wife Larissa, daughter of the Thessalian Piasus. These genealogical stories appear to corroborate the Thessalian origin of the Pelasgi who occupied Cyzicus. Conon further relates that Cyzicus had no successor, and that the Tyrrheni (Pelasgi) took possession of the Cyzicene Chersonnese, subjugating the earlier Thessalians. Still among the mist of mythical events we next come across the Argonauts on their way to Colchis. On landing at Cyzicus they were kindly received by the inhabitants, but after leaving and being driven back on the coast during the night, they were mistaken for enemies, and in the ensuing fight Cyzicus was slain by Jason or Heracles. His death was mourned by the Argonauts as well as by his own people, and his wife Cleite killed herself for grief, the tears of the nymphs originating a fountain which in her memory was called Cleite. During the stay of the Argonauts Hera instigated the giants, who dwelt on Mount Dindymus close by Cyzicus, to destroy Heracles. When Jason and the Argonauts were reconnoitring on the mountain, Briareus and his brother giants threw rocks down upon Heracles, who was left in charge of the ships, and endeavoured to close the mouth of the river Rhyndacus. The rocks were changed by Persephone into an island called Besbicus, and the giants were slain by the arrows of Heracles and his companions. Before leaving the place the Argonauts besought Dindymene for a favourable voyage, and are reported to have erected a temple to Rhea-Cybele, which existed there in after years, together with an image of the goddess, made of the wood of the vine, and like the Artemis at Ephesus and Dionysus of Naxos, no doubt a primitive agalma. As might be looked for, some of the coin-types have reference to Jason and other heroes of the Argonautic myth.

Passing onwards to later times, we arrive at what may be considered the historical origin of the city, in the advent of a colony from Miletus, actuated, it is said, by an oracle from Apollo. This apparently took place, though different dates are given, in Ol. vi. 1, B.C. 756. According to an inscription of Roman times, four of the six tribes into which the Cyzicenes were divided were of

Athenian origin, coming from the Asiatic settlement of Miletus.[1] Another colony is said to have come from Megara, about a century later, in B.C. 675. From this time until the extension of the Lydian kingdom under Gyges, nothing appears to be known of Cyzicus. It came to some extent under the Lydian power when that was carried up to the Hellespont, including the whole of the north of Mysia and almost all the coast from Adramyteum to the Rhyndacus. Though it may be disputed to what extent the Lydian king exercised authority in the time of Gyges, it is clear that Crœsus, by his first invasion of Ionia, made all the Greeks tributary. On the overthrow of the Lydian empire by Cyrus in B.C. 546, and the succeeding conquest of Miletus and other Greek cities in Asia Minor, Cyzicus became subject to Persian rule, and remained in that condition until B.C. 477, when the supremacy of that empire over the Hellenic cities of Asia Minor was overthrown. Cyzicus then came, more or less, under Athenian hegemony. It revolted before the battle of Cynossema, B.C. 411, but was, after the defeat of the Spartans there, again brought under the influence of Athens, whose power was farther strengthened by the total defeat at Cyzicus of the Spartan fleet under Mindarus, who fell in the battle, by Alcibiades and the Athenians, B.C. 410. The rule of Athens continued up to B.C. 405, when, at Ægospotami, Lysander, the Spartan commander, destroyed the Athenian fleet, and for the time broke up the thalassocracy of Athens. Sparta then became predominant, and remained so until B.C. 394, when Conon and Pharnabazus defeated Peisander, and slew him in the battle off Cnidus. Freedom was then restored to the

---

[1] Caylus, tom. ii., Pl. 60—62.

various Greek towns of Asia which had been under Spartan authority, and this they retained up to B.C. 387, when, by the provisions of the peace negotiated by Antalcidas, they again submitted to Persia. In this condition Cyzicus remained till, in B.C. 364, it once more came under Athenian hegemony, to be under her rule but a short time, for after the defeat of Athens at Chios, B.C. 357, the Asiatic towns regained their freedom. From this time until B.C. 334, when Alexander conquered Asia Minor, Cyzicus was a free and very flourishing state. It is unnecessary to carry farther the history, for the issue of the electrum coins, with which alone this essay is concerned, had certainly ceased before then.

The inner polity of an Hellenic state cannot be disconnected from the religion professed within it. The state was supposed to have its origin in some one of the deities of the Hellenic Olympus, or to be the offspring of the prompting or leadership of a god or of some other being in close relationship to him. Its medium of exchange in the shape of money was, therefore, in one sense an outcome of its religion, and received its authentication from a religious sanction. According to Dr. Ernst Curtius, so great an influence had the religion of the state upon its coinage, that it was issued from the temples, and was the νόμισμα of the god therein worshipped rather than of the civic community, if, indeed, in early times the god and the state can be separated. The temples were, on account of the offerings and bequests, and from other sources, the great receptacles of property, the banks in fact of the time, and were therefore under the most favourable circumstances for becoming the issuers of money, and to profit by the transaction. A somewhat similar position was occupied by the great religious houses of the Middle Ages, which accumulating wealth by offerings made to the shrines of saints and for masses, were enabled through the possession of money to become lenders of it, and so in the end, by obtaining mortgages upon land, to become its owners.

The authentication of the currency being, therefore, a religious privilege, whether the money was issued from the temple treasuries or from the mint of the state, the designs on the coins, which were the tokens of its being of a certain weight and quality, were symbols associated in one way or another with the deity whose temples were within the limits of the state. The symbol, therefore, which constituted the badge or arms of the state, was in every sense a religious one, and signified that the city was under the protection of the divinity with whom the symbol was connected. To give a single well-known example, the coins of Athens, from the earliest to the latest period of its independence, bore on one face the head of Athena, and on the other the owl and olive-spray, both so intimately connected with her. The coin-types, therefore, of a Greek state usually bear upon them the impress of the religious cults of the state. In the case of Cyzicus, however, the coin-types do not appear to have been selected with the same rigid adherence to local worship as in most Hellenic cities, though the practice had still a certain and even considerable influence upon the coinage. It will be desirable, therefore, to give a short account of the various cults which, as we learn from historical relation, prevailed at Cyzicus.

The city was provided with a large number of temples, witnessing to the skill of its architects, who were renowned throughout Greece. Cicero (*Pro lege Manilia*) tells us that Cyzicus was one of the most beautiful cities of the

Greek world, and according to Strabo, it rivalled the first cities in Asia in size and beauty.[2] Among its buildings the temples ranked as the most beautiful, and in them were honoured nearly the whole of the gods and goddesses of the Hellenic Pantheon. It is not impossible that the large and wide connection which Cyzicus had with the trading communities of various countries may have been the means of introducing some of their cults into the state, and that as she derived many of her coin-types from the currency of other cities, so she may also have adopted their peculiar gods and worship.

Among the divinities worshipped at Cyzicus, one of the most popular was Cybele, the Magna Mater of Phrygia, who ultimately became merged in the Hellenic Rhea, the mother of the gods, herself probably of Oriental origin. Her worship was introduced at an early period from Phrygia, and she was known at Cyzicus under the name Dindymene, from the mountain Dindymus, in Phrygia, which had its counterpart in another Dindymus close by Cyzicus. She also appears under the name Lobrina, from the mountain Lobrinion, and Placiana, from a town, Placia, where she had a shrine, near Cyzicus. A legend tells us that her worship was brought into Mysia and the Troad by Dardanus. The worship of Rhea appears to have been carried into the Troad and the district about Mount Ida at an equally early period, and Mysia seems to be the country where the two myths, the Phrygian and Hellenic, became united in one.

In intimate association with Cybele is Atys, the shepherd changed into a pine, a tree which, keeping its verdure through the winter, is a fitting emblem of the vivifying

---

[2] Book xii. p. 71.

influence of the sun, with whom Atys may perhaps be identified. He appears to occupy much the same position in regard to Cybele as Alexander-Paris does to Aphrodite, who again, in her Oriental aspect as Astarte, comes into very close relationship with Cybele, as Atys does with Adonis. The Phrygian goddess especially associated with mountains, where her images, many of them unhewn stones, probably acrolites, were most frequently placed, as the great goddess of the wild, is usually accompanied by the lion. She is represented in a car drawn by lions, or seated on a throne with a lion on each side.[3] She usually wears the turreted crown, and the pine-tree was sacred to her. Herodotus relates that when Anacharsis visited the city, there was a great feast held at Cyzicus in honour of this goddess.[4]

Apollo and his sister Artemis are also prominent deities at Cyzicus; and as the father of Cyzicus, no god might seem to have greater claims than Apollo for worship at a city founded by his son. In his capacity, also, of ἀρχηγέτης of the colony from the Ionian city Miletus, Apollo Didymæus was regarded as a second founder of the state.[5] The connection between Cyzicus and Miletus, through the god, appears to have been long maintained, for in the time of Prusias II (B.C. 180—149), Cyzicus gave presents to the temple of Apollo at Miletus.[6] As Lycius, the god of light, he was worshipped at Zeleia, a town in Cyziceno territory, and at Adrastia, as Ἐκβάσιος and Ἀκταῖος, he had an oracle, jointly with Artemis. The

---

[3] In her temple at Cyzicus, under the name Dindymene, there was a marble statue of the goddess between two lions held by her. Zosimus II. 81.

[4] Herod. iv. 76. Clem. Alex. 1715, ed. Potter, vol. i. p. 20.

[5] Aristides, vol. i. p. 388, &c. (Dindorf, 1829.)

[6] Boeckh, *Corp. Inscr. Græc.*, vol. ii. Nos. 2855, 2858.

Hyperborean Apollo naturally has an intimate relation with the city, through the gold which, brought from the regions guarded by his griffins, so abundantly supplied the mint of Cyzicus.

The worship of Artemis may have been brought from Miletus together with that of Apollo, her brother. A feast was held in her honour, and gifts were made to her by the people of Cyzicus, at her temple at Munychia, from which she had one of her names.[7] As λιμενοσκόπος, the harbour-guardian, she was especially and appropriately reverenced at so important a sea-port as Cyzicus.[8] She was also worshipped in Cyzicene territory as Θερμαία, at hot springs on the river Æsepus.[9]

Persephone, equally with Cybele, was worshipped at Cyzicus with peculiar cults and usages. According to Appian,[10] the city was given to her by Zeus as a marriage-gift, and in consequence she was honoured there above all other gods, and a black cow was sacrificed to her, possibly as the wife of Hades, the god of the lower regions, the abode of darkness. Appian tells a story which possesses much picturesque interest. During the siege of the city by Mithradates, the people were reduced to such straits that they were unable to provide a suitable cow to sacrifice to Persephone; they therefore prepared one made of flour as a substitute. And now a marvellous event took place; a black cow swam through the hostile fleet and placed herself in front of the altar ready to be sacrificed. So moved was Mithradates by the incident that he raised the siege, not daring farther to molest a city that

---

[7] Boeckh, vol. ii. No. 3657.
[8] Callimach., *Hymn. in Dianam*, vv. 39, 259.
[9] Aristides, *Orac. Sacr.* iv., vol. i. p. 503 (Dindorf).
[10] *Bellum Mithrad.* vol. i., ed. 1670, p. 871.

was protected by so powerful a goddess.[11] Cyzicus claimed also to be the scene of the rape of Persephone.[12]

Of her mother Demeter historical relation gives but little account in connection with Cyzicus. Nor is anything recorded which enables us to obtain a knowledge of the worship of any of the other gods there, except what Athenæus relates,[13] that there was in the city a statue of Dionysus in the form of a bull.

The Argonautic expedition is the most important myth in connection with the history of Cyzicus, and includes Heracles and the young king Cyzicus, slain through misadventure by the Argonauts. The latter, as the founder, is most intimately associated with the city which bore his name, and there is an inscription which records that a statue was dedicated to him as κτίστης.[14] Games were held in his honour,[15] and his tomb is mentioned by Deilochus.[16]

The importance of Cyzicus as a commercial and trading community began at an early time. Already in the sixth century B.C., if not before, its trade had extended widely, and it became a place whose alliance was sought for by other and distant states. It is true that it was not until a later period that its business intercourse with the Euxine was completely developed, by which it was enabled, besides other lucrative commodities, to draw a large supply of gold on very favourable conditions, through Panticapæum, from the rich metalliferous district

---

[11] Plutarch, in his "Life of Lucullus," also relates that the image of the cow was made of paste, and adds that the sacrifice was acceptable to the goddess.
[12] Propertius, iii., *Eleg.* xxi. *v.* 4.
[13] xi. p. 476, A.
[14] Muratori, p. 1042, 5.
[15] *Apoll. Rhod.* I. 1057 *seq.*
[16] Schol. in *Apoll. Rhod.* I. 1061.

of the Ural Mountains. In no way is its wealth more clearly evidenced than by the large amount of money which it issued, itself a source of profit by no means inconsiderable. This abundance of money is shown not only by the coins themselves, which still remain so numerous and so varied, but by the accounts we possess from various sources, of the large way in which its staters were stored, and how commonly they were in use as a circulating medium over a wide area.

Cyzicus does not appear to have had any silver or gold currency, except a very limited one, during the earlier days of its prosperity; indeed gold never, as in the case of the not distant Lampsacus and Abydus, superseded the earlier electrum coinage.[17] No silver coin is known belonging to a time before the fourth century B.C., except one or two excessively rare pieces, and it appears to be impossible that so few should have come to light if they had ever been systematically issued. It is very difficult to account for this; the more valuable currency of electrum might be sufficient for large commercial purposes and distant trading, but coins of the less valuable metal would be required, it might have been expected, for the ordinary home trade of the state.

Throughout the long period during which Cyzicus issued an electrum coinage one standard only was in use, the Phocaic.[18] It consisted of three denominations, the

---

[17] A Daric, which has the prow of a ship on the reverse, may possibly have been struck at Cyzicus during the satrapy of Pharnabazus, but it cannot be considered as a coin of Cyzicus itself.

[18] The Phocaic standard, the stater of which had a maximum weight of 256 grs., appears to have been based on the Babylonic gold standard, the sixtieth of that mina being 260 grs. Head, *Num. Chron.* N.S., vol. xv. p. 282.

stater, hecta or sixth, and the half-hecta or twelfth. The stater, though it sometimes rose as high as 252 grs., may be considered to average as its highest weight 248 grs., the hecta 41 grs., and the twelfth about 20 grs. There appears to have been a coinage of double staters, but the issue must have been small and probably quite abnormal, for no such coin has yet been discovered. The evidence for its existence is contained in the schedule of the Treasury of Athena in the Parthenon, where, in the list for Ol. lxxxix. 3, B.C. 422 and succeeding years, there is mention made of τετράδραχμον χρυσοῦν of the weight of 500·6 grs., which is just the double of a stater of quite full weight.[19]

The metal of which the Cyzicenes are composed is what was called electrum, or white gold, and consists of gold and silver in combination. That used at Cyzicus is of a deeper colour than that of the early electrum coins of the Asiatic standard, attributed to Miletus, Ephesus, Cyme, Samos, &c., and, though varying to a great extent in that respect, it never approaches the colour of pure gold, such as the gold of the staters classed to Sardes in the time of Crœsus, or of the Darics. No Cyzicene stater has, so far as I am aware, been analysed, and it is therefore impossible to say what are the exact proportions of the metals of which they are composed. The specific gravity has, however, been taken of about half-a-dozen staters of different types, by which it appears that the proportion of

---

[19] *Inscr. Atticæ*, Kirchhoff, vol. i. pp. 61, 62, Nos. 165, 166, 170, 171, 173. A coin-weight of bronze first published by Caylus and afterwards by Lenormant (*Rev. Num.* N. S. vol. i. p. 7), has upon it with a tunny the inscription **KYΞI ΔIC**, which latter he expands into διστάτηρον. It weighs 29·90 gram., which, allowing for loss by oxidation, is just the weight of a double stater.

gold to silver varies very greatly in different specimens. The following are the exact figures:

|  | $N$ per cent. | $R$ per cent. |
|---|---|---|
| Satyr holding tunny | 52·25 | 47·75 |
| Boar l. on tunny | 52 | 48 |
| Lion with fore-paw raised, on tunny | 39 | 61 |
| Head of Pallas on tunny (archaic style) | 38·48 | 61·52 |
| Head of Ammon on tunny | 38·44 | 61·56 |
| Dionysus recumbent l. on panther's skin; beneath, tunny | 27 | 73 [20] |

It also seems certain that the metal is an artificial and not a natural alloy. Gold is, however, sometimes found which has a native alloy of silver combined with it, and it is quite possible that some of the earlier issues of electrum coins may have been struck in native electrum. For instance, the metal of the early Lydian coinage was very probably obtained from the sand of the river Pactolus or from the mines of Mounts Tmolus or Sipylus. Analysis has shown the proportion of gold to silver in this case to be about three to one. Some of the electrum coins of the Asiatic standard, of Miletus and other towns, already referred to, may also have been struck in the same native electrum. But even among the early electrum coins, as of Ephesus, there are some so pale in colour as scarcely to be distinguished from silver except by their weight, which shows them to be adjusted to a divisional system other than that used in the silver coinage of the state to which they belong. These coins can only be the production of an artificial admixture of the two metals, for no gold is

---

[20] For further details see K. B. Hofmann, *Num. Zeit.*, 1884, p. 33, and F. Hultsch, *Zeit. f. Num.*, 1884, p. 165.

found in a natural state which has so large a quantity of silver in alloy as these in question must possess.

In the case of Cyzicus there cannot be much doubt that the greater part, if not the whole, of the electrum used in the coinage of its staters and hectæ was an artificial product and not of natural origin. Gold is not often found in the condition of electrum, and the principal source of supply of that peculiar metal must to a great extent have been worked out before the large issue of Cyzicenes began. There would therefore be a difficulty in obtaining a sufficient quantity of the requisite quality without manufacturing it from purer gold. The most abundant supply of gold for the Cyzicene mint, as we have reason to believe, came from a district—the Ural Mountains—where the metal is of such a nature that to make it of the quality of the staters would require the addition of silver.

The question whether the electrum money was intended to pass current for gold or not has also been a subject of controversy. If the electrum staters and hectæ were issued as gold coins, a large profit must have been gained by the transaction, as the price paid for the alloyed metal must have been much less than that paid for the pure. They certainly possessed one advantage over gold coins in the increased hardness gained by the addition of silver, and the consequent saving in wear and tear. That they were meant to circulate as coins of pure gold appears to be improbable. At the time they were being issued the people among whom they were current were accustomed to gold as applied to decorative purposes and for ornaments. And during at least a part of the time when the Cyzicenes were among the most important of the coins in use in commerce, other coins of pure gold, such as the Darics, and staters of Lampsacus, were equally circulating as trade mediums. People must therefore have been well acquainted with the two metals and quite able to discriminate between them. It must, I think, be regarded as almost a certainty that the electrum coins had a value of their own, different from what they would have possessed if they had been gold coins of the same weight. On the other hand, they are described in the account of the Surveyors of Public Works at Athens, B.C. 434, as χρυσοῦ στατῆρες Κυζικηνοί, Cyzicene gold staters,[21] and after the same fashion in other public accounts at Athens during the later part of the fifth century.[22] In one instance, in the schedule of treasures τῶν ἄλλων θεῶν, in the year B.C. 429, they are classed with Δαρεικοῦ χρυσίου στατῆρες (the Daric being of pure gold), and with Phocæan hectæ of electrum.[23]

The monetary value of the Cyzicene stater is a question of much difficulty. We gather, however, that, at the time of the retreat of the Ten Thousand, it was estimated higher than the Daric, for in B.C. 400 the soldiers were promised, presumably as increased pay, a Cyzicene a month, what they had received previously having been no doubt a Daric.[24] We have, however, more exact information of the value of the Cyzicenes towards the latter part of the fourth century. Demosthenes, in his speech against Phormion, says that the stater of Cyzicus was at that time, about B.C. 335, worth twenty-eight silver Attic drachms in Bosphorus, the same value as in B.C. 434 a gold didrachm, weighing 130 grs., obtained at Athens.[25] They had, perhaps, before the end of the fourth century become deteriorated in value

---

[21] *Inscr. Atticæ*, Kirchhoff, vol. i. p. 158, No. 301, *seq.*
[22] *L.c.* vol. i. p. 79, No. 180, *seq.*
[23] *L.c.* vol. i. p. 90, No. 199.
[24] Xenophon, *Anab.* v. 6, 23 ; vii. 3, 10.
[25] *Inscr. Atticæ*, Kirchhoff, vol. i. p. 160.

from what they had been at its commencement. In the meanwhile there had entered into commerce the large issues of the staters of Philip of Macedon, coined in various places in his kingdom from the gold of the rich mines of Philippi. This abundance of coins in the pure metal would almost necessarily reduce the Cyzicenes to the same value, circulating as the Philips did in the same countries where before then the Cyzicenes to a great extent had a monopoly.

Whatever the precise value of the Cyzicene stater may have been during the period when it was being issued, it formed for more than a century, from B.C. 500, the principal currency for trading purposes of the cities on the shores of the Euxine and of the Ægean Seas. The only other large coins of gold, whether in a pure state or alloyed with silver, were the electrum staters of Lampsacus and the Darics. Phocæa, Lesbos, and other states, not easily identified, though issuing numerous coins of electrum, struck, it seems, none of a higher denomination than hectæ, for no stater that can be attributed to these places is known. The earlier issues of electrum of the sixth, or possibly of the seventh, century had long ceased to be used in commerce, and the gold coinage of Lampsacus, Clazomenæ, Rhodes, &c., had not come into existence. Nor had Athens or Panticapæum at that time adopted a gold currency.

That the issue of staters by Cyzicus was very large is shown by the number of coins of various types which are now known, though so few had come to light in the time of Eckhel that he doubted if the stater of Cyzicus was ever anything more than money of account. But in addition to the coins themselves we have the evidence of Treasury lists and accounts of expenditure at Athens, which show how common was the coin during the fifth century, and how important an element it was in the commercial dealings of that time. It did not require the satirical remark of Eupolis in his comedy (Πόλεις), ἥδε Κύζικος πλέα στατήρων, to tell us how abundant were the Cyzicenes at the time he wrote.

A large supply of gold was needed to furnish the mint at Cyzicus with metal for its coinage, and it is not easy to ascertain the source whence, in the earliest period of the issue of the staters, it was obtained. Gold is found in considerable abundance in several parts of Asia Minor, and it is probable that Cyzicus may have obtained some of the raw metal from these places. The rich mines of Thrace and Macedon, so prolific in the reigns of Philip and Alexander, may also have supplied other portions. Nor is it impossible that trading relations may have even then been established with Panticapæum, though Athens jealously guarded her interests there. In the later period of the issues of Cyzicenes there can be little doubt that the principal source of supply was the district of the Ural Mountains, the gold of which passed to Cyzicus through the market of Panticapæum. The commerce of the Euxine had no doubt been kept by Athens in her own hands as far as was possible; but even before she lost the hegemony which had for many years been hers, Cyzicus had traded in those waters, and to the same port. M. Charles Lenormant appears to think that it was only after the defeat of Athens in Sicily in B.C. 413, and the victory of Sparta over her at Ægospotami in B.C. 405, that the monopoly of the gold from the Urals was lost to Athens and came into the hands of Cyzicus. This opinion is to some extent influenced by his belief that the Cyzicenes belong in the main to the fourth century, an opinion which I think cannot be maintained. Whether Cyzicus obtained gold from Panticapæum before the declension of the power of Athens, as I believe she did, or not, it is certain that for many years that place was a principal centre of supply. It is enough to mention that several finds of Cyzicene staters have taken place near Kertch to show the trade connection between the two states, a connection which was a very profitable one for Cyzicus. It is evident that gold, as indeed might be expected, was of less than its ordinary value at Panticapæum, from the fact that the stater of that city was considerably in excess of the ordinary weight, rising as high as 140 grains. In further proof of the low price of gold there, M. Charles Lenormant (*Rev. Num.*, vol. xx. p. 29) has shown that, whilst in Greece the proportionate value of gold to silver was as one to ten, at Panticapæum it was as one to seven. Such a condition was, therefore, most favourable to Cyzicus, which bought gold there at a price much less than that current in Greece, and benefited largely by the exchange. Cyzicus was not likely to go beyond so favourable a market, and it may be considered as certain that she received, at all events during the later period of the issue of the staters, the greater part of the gold required for her mint from Panticapæum. The gold which we suppose Cyzicus obtained through this channel from the Urals has proved, by analysis of the metal from Siberia by M. C. Rose, to contain, as a maximum, sixteen parts of silver and a trace of copper, out of a hundred, a little less than one-fifth, a proportion of silver much less than what the electrum of the staters undoubtedly possesses. There must, therefore, have been a further addition of silver made before the staters and hectæ were issued from the mint of Cyzicus.

One of the most important subjects in connection with the electrum currency of Cyzicus is that of the types which occur upon its coins. It affords the most valuable and largest illustrations we possess of the various cults which prevailed there. This is, however, to some extent modified by the habit at Cyzicus of copying the types of other states, a practice which will be more fully considered later on. There is no Greek state which produced so many and such varied types as did the city of staters upon its electrum coinage. The series upon the coins of Abdera is doubtless a very extensive and interesting one, but it falls short of the number upon the coins of which I treat. [May I be allowed to express a hope that some one will undertake an account of the coins of Abdera. No more acceptable work could be offered to numismatic science.] Before, however, giving a description of the different types, and attempting to divide them, as far as is possible, into their several classes, it will be necessary to give a general account of the coins in question.

It has been already mentioned that the whole of the electrum currency of Cyzicus was struck after one standard, the Phocaic, but it is divided into two very distinct coinages, both in respect of date and appearance. The earliest one comprised, it appears, a single issue, of which, so far as I know, a single specimen is known. It is the stater No. 1, and differs from all the other electrum coins of Cyzicus, not only in the form of the incuse of the reverse, which is most distinct from that of the general body of the Cyzicenes, but also in the subject of the obverse, which separates itself from the ordinary features of the staters in general, though perhaps the stater No. 161 may appear to have something in common with it. Different though it is, there can be no doubt that it is a coin of Cyzicus; the weight and the type afford sufficient grounds for attributing it to that state without hesitation. The type contains, as its principal part, the badge or arms (ἐπίσημον) of Cyzicus, the tunny fish (πηλάμυς), a very valuable product of the Propontis, where enormous numbers were captured on their migratory passage, backwards and forwards, between the Euxine and the Ægean Seas. This badge—and upon the stater in question it is the principal type—continued to be placed on the money of Cyzicus, as a subordinate though distinguishing symbol, during the whole issue of her electrum currency.

The second and long-continued coinage of electrum money, which bears upon it, as I have just stated, the tunny as a subordinate symbol, has for the principal type on the obverse a large number of very varied subjects. The reverse, however, throughout the entire period of the several issues, consists of an incuse (Pl. I. 1 A, 1 B) to which, on account of its resemblance to that apparatus, the name of mill-sail has very appropriately been given. This incuse, while retaining its general form, varies considerably, and markedly in one particular. The two sunken parts of the mill-sail pattern in many of the coins have a plain surface (1 A), while in others, and they belong to the later issues, the surface is granulated (1 B), or has short raised lines upon it.

The name of the city is not found upon a single electrum coin, and indeed upon one alone (No. 54) is there any inscription at all. Though there is nothing in the shape of a name by which to class these coins to Cyzicus, the presence of the tunny upon them is sufficient for their attribution, just as the seal (phoca) upon certain hectæ enables us to give those coins to Phocæa. Upon some of the silver coins, however, the name of the city is to be

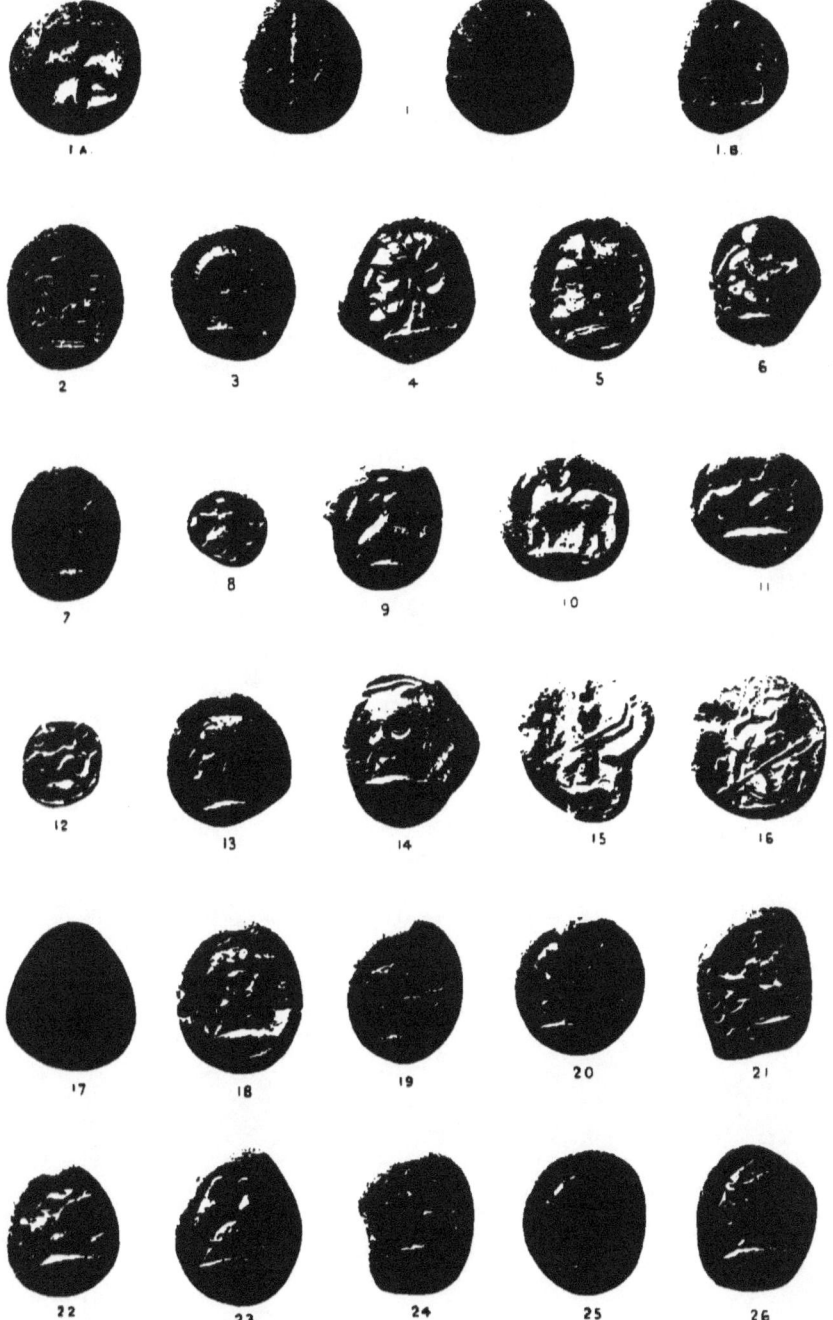

found, together with the tunny, and upon a coin-weight of bronze, already noticed, first published by Caylus and afterwards by M. Charles Lenormant,[26] the tunny and the name of the city are both present.

In considering the types it will be necessary, in the first place, to make an attempt to classify them according to their subjects, and to attach them to the several gods or myths to which they appear to belong; and, secondly, to trace those types which seem to be of foreign origin to the states from whose coinage they have been copied, or from which, on account of the subject, they appear to have been adopted. Both these inquiries have, to some extent, been carried out in the separate account of the various coins; but it seems desirable to make a more systematic classification than could be made under the head of each type.

In connection with the types it is necessary to state that it is highly probable that the subject upon each stater was also produced upon the smaller denominations of the same issue. It is impossible, with our present imperfect material, to change this probability into a certainty, but there are so many cases where staters and the subordinate parts have the same type upon them, that I believe it is only because so many coins are at present lost to us that we do not possess the full complement of stater, hecta and twelfth of every type.[27]

To commence, then, with the great gods of the Olympian hierarchy :

To Zeus may be attributed with certainty the figure with eagle, No. 2, and the heads of Zeus-Ammon, Nos. 3, 4,

---

[26] *Rev. Num.* N.S., vol. i. p. 7, Pl. I. 2.

[27] A table of all the types, showing in each case the denominations at present known, will be found at the end of the introduction.

and possibly the staters with an eagle, Nos. 151 to 153, though No. 151 may be merely a copy, somewhat varied, of a coin of Elis or of Agrigentum, and Nos. 152, 153 may be symbols of Helios.

To Poseidon may be attributed with certainty Nos. 5 to 8, and Nos. 9, 10, in connection with his son Taras, though here we have direct copies of two Tarentine types. Triton, No. 11, may also be classed to Poseidon, though he has an individuality of his own. The horse, No. 126, the dolphin, No. 157, and the pistrix, No. 169, cannot well be separated from Poseidon, though Apollo has a claim to the dolphin; and the strange types from No. 158 to No. 168, including the crab, No. 159, and the shell, No. 160, appear to fall into the same category.

To Demeter may be attributed Nos. 12 to 15, and the stater with Triptolemus, No. 16, must be included in the same class.

To Apollo, as might be expected, a large number of coins may be attributed. Direct representations of the god are found upon Nos. 17 to 21, and the omphalos, No. 22, and the lyre, No. 172, are both in the closest connection with him. Helios, No. 23, the sun-god, represents the Oriental side of his attributes, and the head placed on a disk, No. 77, is possibly one of Helios. The griffin of Apollo occurs on Nos. 143 to 150, though these types may originate in coins of Teos, Abdera, or Panticapæum. The dolphin, No. 157, was sacred to him, but Poseidon has, perhaps, the better claim.

Artemis does not occur herself, but she is represented by the head of Actæon, No. 24.

Pallas is not found, except in representations of her head, Nos. 25 to 29, if all of these are heads of the goddess. The very strange head, No. 30, cannot be one of Pallas, but may possibly, if a Gorgon-head, be connected with her. Gaia, No. 31, and Cecrops, No. 32, portions of a group where Athena receives Erichthonius as his protector, naturally fall into the same series of Pallas subjects, which may also include Harmodius and Aristogeiton, No. 76, since Pallas and Athens are inseparable.

Aphrodite is certainly represented, and accompanied by Eros on No. 34, and, somewhat doubtfully, in the head, No. 33.

Of Hermes there is only the head, No. 35, though the goat, Nos. 133, 134, may have its place on the coins in connection with him, Dionysus, however, having as good a claim.

No other of the Olympian deities appear on the electrum coins of Cyzicus, but the Great Mother, though only appearing in one instance, No. 55, in her own person, and once again through the head of Atys, No. 56, is very fully represented by the lion, Nos. 103 to 117, though it is quite possible that in many, if not in all of these types, it is not in connection with Cybele that the lion occurs.

Among the gods of a lower rank, Dionysus is by far the most frequently found on the coinage of Cyzicus. He occurs himself on Nos. 36 to 39. In connection with him and his rites we have the head of Pan, No. 40, the centaur, No. 46, and satyrs, in one or other aspect, on Nos. 41 to 44, and a satyric mask, No. 45, and a bifrontal head, No. 47. The ass, No. 129, probably belongs to him, and the fox, No. 142, was sacred to Bassareus, the Lydian Dionysus.

Asclepius may be represented, though it is very doubtful, through the fore part of the cock on No. 155 and the cock's head on No. 156.

A Nereid, or Thetis, appears on No. 48, and the type on No. 49 is distinctly Scylla.

River gods occur in the form of a man-headed bull on Nos. 50, 51, though the latter may have no connection with any river near Cyzicus, being a perfect copy of the ordinary coins of Gela.

Nike is represented on Nos. 52, 53, on the first stater, in commemoration of a naval victory; and Eleutheria, with her name attached, occurs on No. 54.

The voyage of the ship Argo and the myth connected therewith, interwoven into the legendary history of Cyzicus, introduces us to Heracles, who is represented on Nos. 62 to 69; and on No. 141 we have Cerberus, whom he chained in Hades.

It is quite possible that Jason is the warrior who is adjusting his arrow before fitting it to the bow on Nos. 93, 94, and the Scythian archer, No. 95, may have reference to the voyage to Colchis. With either Jason or Helle, the ram on Nos. 130 to 132 was very probably associated, and there cannot be much doubt that the prow on No. 170 is of the ship Argo.

Perseus himself occurs on No. 74, and his head on No. 73, and in connection with him there is the Gorgon-head on No. 75. Bellerophon, another solar hero, brings in the Chimæra on Nos. 119, 120, and also Pegasus on No. 127, though it probably occurs as a copy of the common type of Corinth.

Odysseus appears to have the best claim, though it is disputed, to the head on No. 70, and to be the warrior killing the ram on No. 71. Nor do I think there can be any doubt that the suppliant by the omphalos on No. 72 is Orestes. And the head on No. 80 is quite possibly of the native hero Cyzicus.

A large number of types still remain which it is difficult to assign to any special god, hero, or myth, some of them possibly connected with Oriental cults. Among these are several heads, male and female, as Nos. 78, 79, 81 to 84; winged human figures, Nos. 58, 59, 61, and a winged lion-headed man, No. 57, possibly Fear (Φόβος). There are also several human figures, carrying the tunny, Nos. 86, 87, 88, 89; on the stater and hecta, No. 88, holding also a knife; carrying a helmet on No. 90, and holding a shield, Nos. 91, 92. Then again there are harpies, sphinxes, bulls, swine, and dogs, which it would be hazardous to allot, and which I prefer to leave to the ingenious speculation of persons more imaginative than myself.

The question arises with regard to the subjects on the staters which can be appropriated to gods or myths, whether they are derived from gods worshipped at Cyzicus and to local myths, or from gods and myths belonging more especially to other places. It is impossible to decide this question with any degree of certainty. But there can be no doubt whatever that Cyzicus adopted subjects belonging to cults foreign to her and placed them on her coinage. She appears to have followed this practice much more freely than did any other state; indeed, it is one almost peculiar to herself. For the reason of this we must probably look to the wide-spread commercial intercourse her citizens had with places where gods and cults prevailed, strange to herself, and in some cases strange even to Hellas itself. It may well have happened that persons of importance in the state, and connected, as magistrates, with the coinage, had intimate relations of one kind or another with foreign and even far-distant places. Such persons may have sought to distinguish that connection by placing upon the coinage of their own city, types selected from coins of the states with which they were holding intercourse; or the state itself of Cyzicus may have wished to ingratiate itself or conciliate by such a process other states with which it was connected by trade or treaty. This appears to be illustrated by the subjects on some of the staters which have a direct reference to Athens, a state with which Cyzicus held the most intimate relations, even to the extent of being for many years, during the period of the electrum issue, under her hegemony. But Cyzicus carried the practice of placing on her coinage subjects connected with other states and their religions still farther. Many of the staters are direct copies of the coins of other places, the only difference between the two types being the introduction of the tunny upon the Cyzicenes. An examination of the plates will at once show the coins just referred to, but it may be useful to place them specifically before the reader in order that they may be the more readily distinguished.

The two staters, Nos. 9, 10, are identical in all essential points with well-known and common didrachms of Tarentum. Apollo holding a bow and watching the effect of the arrow he has just discharged, No. 18, occurs on a hemi-obol of Sicyon. Perhaps no one of the heads of Pallas can be regarded as a direct copy of her head on the money of Athens, but the head of Pan, No. 40, is so like that on the coins of Panticapæum, that the one must almost certainly have been taken from the other. The forepart of the human-headed bull, No. 51, might have come from the mint at Gela, but for the metal of which it is composed and the tunny upon it. The head of Odysseus, No. 70, is an exact counterpart of that on a gold coin of Lampsacus, but it is difficult to say which is the prototype. The beautiful female head, No. 85, is a close copy of one on a tetradrachm of Syracuse. The lioness devouring, No. 109, finds a counterpart in an archaic coin, of which many have been found in Italy and near Marseilles, but which is probably from the mint of Phocæa. The lion's scalp, No. 113, though differently treated, is similar to the ordinary type of Samos. The two bulls, Nos. 121 and 122, the one standing, the other butting, are so like to the same animal on the coins of Poseidonia and Thurium, that they cannot be regarded in any other light than as copies, and the same may be said of Pegasus, No. 127, in relation to Corinth. The sow, No. 136, is identical with one on an early electrum stater of the Asiatic standard of uncertain attribution, and the forepart of a winged boar, No. 137, is very like that on the coins of Clazomenæ. The Chimæra, No. 120, bears a strong resemblance to the same monster on an early electrum coin of the Phocaic standard, attributed by Mr. Head to Zeleia. The griffin, No. 144, must have been executed by an artist who had before him, in his mind's eye at least, the kindred creatures of Teos or Abdera, and the eagle, No. 151, is the same bird as that of Elis, while that on No. 153, is essentially one with the eagle on an electrum coin of the Asiatic standard, attributed to Abydos. Other coins might, perhaps, be added to this list, but those above referred to are the most evident copies.

The varied character and the large number of types on the electrum coinage of Cyzicus may, perhaps, be accounted for by the long period during which these coins were issued, and, no doubt, with some modifications, this was one cause of the diversity of types. Where the practice of placing a mark on the coin, to designate the magistrate under whose authority the coin was issued, was in use, and when that practice had prevailed over a long period of time, it follows as a necessary consequence that the coins should present a large number of these distinguishing marks.

As a rule these marks were subordinate to the symbols forming the badge of the state, which usually occupied the most prominent position on the coin. At Cyzicus, however, a quite different custom prevailed; the magisterial device became there the principal subject on the coin, the badge of the state occupying a secondary position. In relation to the annual issue of coin-types at Cyzicus, M. Six has argued,[28] and with much force, that each type denotes the coin-issue for one year, under the authority and containing the distinctive mark of the magistrate in authority for that year. Mr. Head dissents from this opinion, and I think on just grounds. The art style of the coins is the best, indeed, almost the sole evidence we possess in regard to their date, for we have scarcely any help from history, and, in the absence of inscriptions, we have no aid from letter-forms. Judging, then, by their style, if we accept M. Six's theory we should, in my opinion, be compelled to compress far too large a number of different coins into a given period than would be possible if only a single type had been issued in each year. We may agree, I think, with Mr. Head that it is "more probable that several, perhaps numerous, types were in use at one and the same time." As the superabundance of coins of different types during a given period is one objection to M. Six's view, so the paucity of coins during other periods may also be urged against it. This, however, is a much less valid objection than the first, because we cannot tell how many types

---

[28] *Num. Chron.* N.S., vol. xvii. p. 171.

which are now entirely lost to us may have been issued from the mint of Cyzicus.

When we come to the consideration of the time during which the electrum coinage of Cyzicus was in course of issue, we are left without any direct evidence from historical relation, and are, therefore, obliged in the main to judge from the coins themselves, their fabric and their art. At first sight they might appear, on account of their thick and lumpy appearance and the nature of the reverse, to be much earlier than they are. These features are, however, merely survivals, and, like the archaic head of Pallas on the later coins of Athens, were probably retained by Cyzicus on account of trade requirements. The incuse on the reverse was kept up at Cyzicus long after its use had ceased in all other places except at Phocæa, where it is equally found on the hectæ of that state. That side of the coin must, therefore, be disregarded in the consideration of date, and the obverse with its type-subject must alone be our guide.

The stater, No. 1, already referred to, separates itself from all the other electrum coins of Cyzicus, not only by the difference of its reverse, but by the time of its issue. It is certainly much earlier than any of the electrum coins of what may be designated as the second series, and may be attributed to the first part of the sixth century B.C., if it is not as early as B.C. 600. It stands quite alone as the sole representative of the earliest coinage of the state.

For a period of almost a century Cyzicus does not seem to have had any currency. The Lydian gold coinage during that time probably supplied the commercial requirements of the Greek states of Asia Minor. Cyzicus had not then attained the wealth and importance of which she afterwards became possessed.

Some time about the year B.C. 500 Cyzicus appears to have commenced the issue of the celebrated χρυσοῦ στατῆρες Κυζικηνοί, together with the smaller denominations, hectæ, and half-hectæ or twelfths, with which she was for many years to be identified, and which made her one of the richest cities of Asia Minor. That the first issue of this series could not have taken place much, if at all, later than B.C. 500 is shown by the style exhibited upon some of the staters. For instance, the figures, Nos. 59, 61, have all the characteristics of a very early date, one, possibly, still earlier than that specified as the commencement of the second series of coinage. The whole of the curious coins from No. 157 to No. 168, many of them with the fish-head, including the stater, No. 161, also appear to be rather before than after B.C. 500. Nos. 150, 154, may also be included in the same class. A little later than these, but still belonging to quite the archaic period, which Mr. Head proposes to close at B.C. 480, are the head of Pallas, No. 25, with the head in profile, but having the eye as if seen in front; the heads, Nos. 26, 27, 77, 78; the strange head, No. 30; the Satyric mask, No. 45; the bifrontal head, No. 47; the Gorgon head, No. 75; and the helmet, No. 171; Triton, No. 11; the Satyr, No. 41; the human-headed bull, No. 50; the lion-headed winged man, No. 57; the running figure, No. 58, and the two winged figures, Nos. 59, 61; Heracles with club and bow, No. 65; figure holding two tunnies, No. 87; the Harpies and the Sphinxes, Nos. 97 to 102; the forepart of lioness, No. 109; the forepart of lion, No. 110; the Chimæra, Nos. 119, 120; and the forepart of a winged boar, No. 137.

To a period not long after B.C. 480, may perhaps be attributed the head of Perseus, No. 73; the heads, Nos.

79, 84; figure holding tunny and knife, No. 88; the griffin, No. 145; the forepart of cock, No. 155; and the pistrix, No. 169.

Without attempting any classification of them in detail we may regard a large proportion of the remaining coins as belonging to a period between B.C. 440 and B.C. 410. Among the coins which appear to have been issued during this interval may perhaps be included: The human heads, Nos. 3, 5, 17, 18, 21, 24, 28, 30, 36, 62, 73, 75, 80, 84, 85; the figures, Nos. 2, 6, 7, 8, 9, 10, 14, 16, 19, 23, 31, 32, 39, 42 to 44, 46, 48, 49, 53, 55, 63, 64, 66 to 69, 71, 72, 74, 86, 89 to 96; animals, 51, 60, 103 to 108, 113, 115, 117, 118, 121 to 127, 129 to 142; birds, 151 to 153, 155; monsters, 143, 144, 146, 148, 149; the prow, 170, and the lyre, 172. The remainder of the types, including Nos. 15, 19 to 21, 34, 38, 52, 54, 76, may be attributed to the time between B.C. 410 and the accession of Philip to the throne of Macedon, B.C. 359. Among the coins of the last class are some human heads, Nos. 12, 13, 33, 37, 81 to 83, which in the opinion of persons of high authority were struck not much, if at all, earlier than the time of Alexander. With every deference for this opinion I feel obliged to dissent from it, and to regard these coins, though, perhaps, belonging to the latest of the staters, as having been issued not later than B.C. 360. The conclusion, therefore, at which I have arrived with regard to the Cyzicenes is, that with the exception of No. 1, they all belong to the time between the year B.C. 500, or possibly a little earlier, and the year B.C. 360.

M. François Lenormant, holding the same view as his father, in the last account he has given of the Cyzicenes,[29]

---

[29] *Dict. des Antiq.* Daremberg and Saglio, under " Cyziceni."

expresses the opinion that the principal issue was between the end of the Peloponnesian War, B.C. 404, and the time of Alexander, who began to reign B.C. 336. M. Six, whose authority is of great value, also considers that some of the staters were issued as late as the time of Alexander's accession.

If it were possible to adopt M. Lenormant's opinion, we should have to cast aside all considerations of style, though it is upon that evidence alone that the question of the date of the staters must be decided. It is, however, an opinion which cannot be entertained, for whatever view may be taken of some of the heads, no one can pretend to say, having regard to the style of the coins, that the greater part were struck after the year B.C. 404. In rejecting M. Six's view, which, however, has reference only to a very few of the staters, I by no means feel the same confidence. It is true, indeed, that the heads, Nos. 12, 13, and especially No. 83 cannot be rejected, on account of their style, as being inconsistent with the date M. Six attributes to them, but on the other hand it cannot be justly asserted that they may not have been struck before B.C. 360. It appears to be on the whole a safer conclusion at which to arrive, that the issue of staters entirely ceased before B.C. 360, than to suppose that, several years after that time, two or three types were struck in an abnormal way and quite out of due course.

The fact that Demosthenes mentions Cyzicenes as a common currency in Bosphorus in his own time has been considered a proof that they were issued as late as then. This evidence is, however, of a very inconclusive kind, since it is certain that a class of coins so largely issued and so widely circulated would continue to be used in commerce and in other ways long after they had ceased to be produced by the mint. It does not need to adduce instances of so trite an occurrence. The same explanation may be given of Cyzicene staters having been found in a vase associated with coins of Alexander, as was the case at the Piræus a few years ago.

It is a fact which is indisputable that for a long period, and over a large area, the Cyzicenes, together with Darics, formed the principal gold currency of the shores of the Ægean and neighbouring seas. This position they held until a coin of purer metal was put into circulation in large quantities, and then when Philip of Macedon issued from numerous mints the stater which bore his name, Cyzicus ceased to enjoy the monopoly which had so long been hers, and the coinage of the Cyzicenes came to an end.

The position Cyzicus occupied in the Hellenic world in regard to art cannot, perhaps, be either fairly or fully estimated from the evidence afforded by its coinage. The process of engraving on a die, leaving out of consideration the limited space on which a subject has to be represented, does not allow that scope for artistic treatment which is granted to painting, to sculpturing in marble, or to casting in bronze. It is bound, like gem engraving, by laws existing within its own province of expression, which it cannot break, and from the control of which the kindred arts are more or less free. Subject, however, to these qualifications, the numerous representations of human and animal form and the way in which the characteristic features of gods and heroes, as well as those of the lower orders of life, are depicted upon the coins, enable us to form an opinion, though it may be an inadequate one, upon the artistic development of prosperous and wealthy Cyzicus.

We know that the school of painting there had produced

artists of eminence, and, though we do not hear so much of its sculptors, there can be little doubt that Cyzicus was not behind other cities of Asia Minor, whose temple decorations and other works of sculpture are still left to testify to the genius and skill of their inhabitants. The site of Cyzicus never having been excavated, we are left without the evidence which has been supplied by an examination of the remains of other cities, such, for instance, as Pergamon, with the sculptures of which place it is not improbable that Cyzicus had much in common.

As has already been stated, the coinage of a state does not afford a complete index of the wealth it possessed in the productions of its sculptors, nor does it indicate, except in an imperfect manner, the height to which at the place in question plastic art had attained. But at Cyzicus we have still less opportunity than at other cities of estimating by means of the coinage the artistic condition there. In most Hellenic states the coin-types were local, the outcome of the religious cults or myths of the place itself, and were influenced not only by the traditional and continuous teaching of the special art-school there, but also by the sentiment begotten of the worship of the gods with whom the city was, in one or other way, connected, and who were its tutelary guardians and protectors, and in some cases its founders. At Cyzicus, on the contrary, the subjects of the coin-types were to a large extent borrowed from other states, and her school of die-engraving was, at all events in the selection of the types, of the most eclectic kind. It is difficult, indeed, to say of many of her coins whether the subject upon them was indigenous to the city or was adopted or adapted from the coinage or sculpture of other and sometimes far-distant states, but that a considerable proportion belong to the latter class is unquestionable. With this limitation in respect of original design, which, however, must not be carried too far, the artists of Cyzicus, who were the engravers of her coin-dies, show great skill and even power in the way in which they have treated the subjects at their disposal. In the separate description of each of the types which is given later on, it is noted from whence the several subjects, which are direct imitations of other coins or are copies of groups in marble, have been derived; but it seems desirable to give here a few instances of coins where such a reproduction has taken place. The staters Nos. 9 and 10, figure riding on dolphin and horseman, are copies of familiar coins of Tarentum. No. 51, forepart of human-headed bull, is the ordinary type of Gela; No. 85, female head, is precisely similar to one on a Syracusan tetradrachm; while Nos. 31 and 32, Gaia and Erichthonius, and Cecrops, are in all respects like to portions of a group in terracotta, itself no doubt copied from one in marble; and No. 76, Harmodius and Aristogeiton, represents a sculptured subject, once a celebrated and popular one at Athens. In the case of these types the artists of the mint of Cyzicus appear as little more than mere copyists, but there are other cases in which they have adopted a subject from a coin of another city but have modified it after their own fashion, showing in the process not only power of adaptation but of invention also. Instances of this may, perhaps, be found in No. 16, Triptolemus in the serpent car; No. 18, Apollo watching the effect of the flight of his arrow; No. 21, Apollo on a swan; No. 63, Heracles and Iphicles; No. 69, Heracles strangling the lion; No. 151, eagle tearing a tunny; and also in the lions, bulls, and griffins of which so many and different representations occur on the staters. In no way, however, have the Cyzicene die-engravers shown their skill more conspicuously than in the manner in which they have adapted the subject to the space at their disposal; their success in this very important feature in the treatment of coin-types evidences much ingenuity and power in the moulding of form. Striking examples of this are shown in No. 38, Dionysus seated; No. 48, Nereid carrying a wreath; Nos. 52 and 54, Nike and Eleutheria; No. 68, Heracles holding club and lion's skin; No. 71, Odysseus slaying a ram; and the staters where warriors and others, satyrs among the rest, are represented in kneeling or bending positions. But they achieved a still greater success than this, for they have dared to make the great gods assume, yet without loss of dignity, the attitude almost of suppliants.

But the die-engravers of Cyzicus were not merely copyists or adapters of the works of other artists, they give evidence upon many of the staters of the faculty of original design. This appears to be as fully expressed in their treatment of Dionysiac types as in any other of the numerous subjects on the coinage, and, indeed, in relation to the currency, Dionysus figures at Cyzicus as a very prominent and popular god. The staters, Nos. 42 to 44, where satyrs are seen in different aspects, are examples of quite novel treatment of those attendants upon Dionysus, and they are examples as successful as they are novel.

It cannot, I think, be denied, after a due examination of the whole series of the electrum coins, that at Cyzicus, notwithstanding the eclectic tendency of its coin-types, due in some respects perhaps to commercial relations, a school of die-engravers was in existence which possessed not only a distinctive character combined with originality, but also much artistic power and skill in expression and adaptation.

The subjects represented on the coins seem to have been derived from many sources. Some are of original design, some are simply copies of other coins, and some are modifications of the types on the coins of other states. There are also others which have been taken from single figures or groups in marble, in whole or in part, and which in some cases have been directly reproduced, while in others they have been changed in a greater or less degree in accordance with the taste or feeling of the artist, or to fit them to the requirement of the space on the coin. All those, however, which are not original designs give indications of the translation they have undergone, and show the impression they have received from passing through the mind and under the hand of the Cyzicene engraver. The prototypes of some of the coin subjects appear to have been separate groups or single statues; but others, and probably the greater number, were portions of scenes which ornamented the friezes and pediments of temples, or in some cases of metopes. If we had the good fortune to be in possession of the sculptures which decorated the temples of Cyzicus and other cities, neighbouring or foreign, we should doubtless find some which would give us the clue to the origin of many of the coin-types.

As might be expected, the greater number of the subjects belong to the cults and myths of Hellas, and we are brought face to face with Zeus, Poseidon, Demeter, Apollo, Pallas, and Aphrodite, Dionysus, Heracles, Odysseus, Orestes, and Perseus, though some of them present an aspect not quite in harmony with their Hellenic relations. There are also a large number which are more or less Oriental in their character. The greater part of these are subjects taken from cults where the ancient Hellenic mythology had become influenced and altered by Eastern systems of religious worship, but a few appear to be even still more directly and purely of Oriental origin.

On a review of the extensive and important series of the Cyzicene electrum coinage, extending as it did through a lengthened period, during which art had developed from almost its first beginnings to the highest perfection it ever attained, we cannot but be struck by the sustained excellence of the monetary art of Cyzicus. No state equalled it in the variety of subjects represented on its coins, as none excelled it in the high artistic qualities with which those subjects were endowed. There are coins, no doubt, among the large range of the money of the various states of Hellas, which surpass any that proceeded out of the mint of Cyzicus, but no state can pretend to equal it in the number and variety of works of such high artistic merit as the staters of Cyzicus present. If the coinage of this great commercial city on the Hellespont is contrasted with that of Athens, a state politically as superior to Cyzicus as its trading enterprises were more widely and largely extended, and which in art was at the head of all Hellenic culture, the difference is indeed marvellous. While the one city was issuing type after type, each one rivalling the other in the beauty and appropriateness of the design and the skill of its execution, the other was reproducing, century after century, almost without any change or advance in style, the same and only type with which she had commenced her monetary issue. The requirements of trade with the "barbarians" has been, and probably with truth, alleged as the reason why Athens, with all her wealth of sculptors and her supremacy in art, continued so long to send out from her mint the uninviting "owl." But there were the same requirements to be considered at Cyzicus, and that she rose superior to these considerations seems to demand from all who admit the claims of art to be a civilising influence, a very high recognition of her merits.

The circumstances attending the discovery of the staters, either of single coins or of a number found deposited together, is a matter of some importance, and we should be much assisted in any inquiry as to the area within which the Cyzicenes circulated, and to some extent also in regard to the time at which certain types were issued, if we were in possession of correct information about the finding of these coins. It is, however, only on rare occasions that anything authentic can be ascertained as to the number, contents, and place of finding of the various hoards which have been brought to light. We are, however, fortunately in possession of fairly trustworthy details connected with two deposits of Cyzicene staters, and also of the places where a few single coins have been found. In the neighbourhood of Kertch, the ancient Panticapæum, several deposits of Cyzicenes have occurred, some, as has been stated, in the numerous and rich tombs with which the locality abounds. No exact account has been given of these finds, and it is believed that the coins were in most cases melted. Some isolated staters have also been met with near Kertch, which have been preserved, and which are noticed in the following account of the staters. Of the two hoards above referred to, both of much importance, I propose to state shortly what is known of their contents.

The first was discovered in the year 1875, not far, it is believed, from the site of Clazomenæ. It consisted of several Darics, many electrum staters of Lampsacus, and a large series of staters of Cyzicus, but no hectæ, nor twelfths. I have found it impossible to ascertain what was the whole number of coins, or the number of each class, but I believe the following list includes the greater part, if not all, of the types of the Cyzicenes.

Nos. 3, 6, 16, 17, 18, 22, 23, 24; [Pl. I., 3, 6, 17, 18, 19, 23, 24, 25]. Nos. 30, 31, 32, 36, 42, 44, 48, 51; [Pl. II., 7, 8, 9, 13, 20, 22, 26, 31]. Nos. 64, 65, 68, 69, 73; [Pl. III., 15, 16, 19, 20, 24]. Nos. 80, 85, 86, 87 ?, 88, 89, 90, 93, 97, 99; [Pl. IV., 1, 7, 8, 9 ?, 10, 12, 13, 16, 23, 27]. Nos. 107, 113, 115, 121, 122, 124, 127, 129, 130, 134; [Pl. V., 1, 6, 8, 15, 16, 18, 21, 23, 24, 29]. Nos. 141, 143, 144, 146; [Pl. VI., 3, 5, 6, 8].

The other discovery was made in 1882 at the Piræus, when about forty to forty-five coins appear to have been found in a terra-cotta vase. The principal part were Cyzicene staters, but there were also some staters of Alexander the Great, but no hectæ nor twelfths. I have been unable to obtain a full account either of the number or of the types of the Cyzicenes, but I believe the following is an almost complete list of the types.

Nos. 9, 24; [Pl. I., 9, 25]. Nos. 29, 43, 48, 50; [Pl. II., 6, 21, 26, 29]. Nos. 63, 64, 67, 72, 76; [Pl. III., 14, 15, 18, 23, 28]. Nos. 99*, 100; [Pl. IV., 29]. Nos. 122, 127, 130, 134; [Pl. V., 16, 21, 24, 29]. No. 141; [Pl. VI., 3].

---

THE FOLLOWING COLLECTIONS ARE REFERRED TO IN AN ABBREVIATED FORM.

British Museum, London—Brit. Mus.
Bibliothèque Nationale, Paris—Paris.
Bibliothèque Nationale, De Luynes—Paris (De L.).
Koenigliches Museum, Berlin—Berlin.
Koenigliche Sammlung, Munich—Munich.
Kaiserliche Sammlung, Vienna—Vienna.
The Imperial Hermitage, St. Petersburg—St. Pet.
The Royal Cabinet, Copenhagen—Copenhagen.
The Royal Cabinet at the Hague—Hague.
Public Numismatic Museum, Athens—Athens.
Herzogliche Sammlung, Gotha—Gotha.
Hunter Collection, Glasgow—Hunter.
Leake Collection, Cambridge—Leake.
Sir Edward Bunbury, Bart., London—Bunbury.
Dr. Weber, London—Weber.
Mr. Thomas Jones, London—Jones.

Lt.-General Moore, London—Moore.
Lord Ashburnham—Ashburnham.
Mr. Arthur J. Evans, Oxford—Evans.
Rev. William Greenwell, Durham—W. G.
Mr. Carfrae, Edinburgh—Carfrae.
M. W. H. Waddington, Paris—Waddington.
The late Baron de Hirsch, Paris—Hirsch.
Dr. Imhoof-Blumer, Winterthur—Imhoof.
M. J. P. Six, Amsterdam—Six.
Herr A. Löbbecke, Brunswick—Löbbecke.
M. Iversen, St. Petersburg—Iversen.
Messrs. Rollin and Feuardent, Paris—R. and F.
M. Hoffmann, Paris—Hoffmann.
Professor Rhousopoulos, Athens—Rhousopoulos.
M. Lambros, Athens—Lambros.

## TABLE OF DENOMINATIONS.

| No. | Stater. | Hecta. | Twelfth. | No. | Stater. | Hecta. | Twelfth. |
|---|---|---|---|---|---|---|---|
| 1 | × | | | 44 | × | | |
| 2 | × | | | 45 | | × | × |
| 3 | × | | | 46 | | × | |
| 4 | × | | | 47 | | × | |
| 5 | × | × | | 48 | × | | |
| 6 | × | | | 49 | × | | |
| 7 | × | | | 50 | × | × | × |
| 8 | | × | | 51 | × | | |
| 9 | × | | | 52 | × | × | |
| 10 | × | | | 53 | | × | |
| 11 | × | × | | 54 | × | | × |
| 12 | × | | | 55 | × | | |
| 13 | × | | | 56 | × | × | |
| 14 | × | | | 57 | × | | |
| 15 | × | | | 58 | × | × | |
| 16 | × | | | 59 | × | | |
| 17 | × | | | 60 | | | × |
| 18 | × | | | 61 | × | | |
| 19 | × | | | 62 | × | | |
| 20 | × | | | 63 | × | × | |
| 21 | × | | | 64 | × | | |
| 22 | × | | | 65 | × | × | |
| 23 | × | × | | 66 | × | | |
| 24 | × | | | 67 | × | | |
| 25 | × | × | × | 68 | × | | |
| 26 | × | × | | 69 | × | | |
| 27 | × | × | | 70 | × | | |
| 28 | × | | | 71 | × | × | |
| 29 | × | | | 72 | × | × | |
| 30 | × | | | 73 | × | × | |
| 31 | × | | | 74 | × | × | |
| 32 | × | × | | 75 | | × | |
| 33 | × | | | 76 | × | | |
| 34 | × | | | 77 | × | × | × |
| 35 | × | | | 78 | × | × | |
| 36 | × | | | 79 | × | | |
| 37 | × | | | 80 | × | | |
| 38 | × | × | | 81 | × | | |
| 39 | × | | | 82 | × | | |
| 40 | × | | | 83 | × | | |
| 41 | × | × | | 84 | × | | |
| 42 | × | | | 85 | × | | |
| 43 | × | | | 86 | × | × | × |

## THE ELECTRUM COINAGE OF CYZICUS.

### TABLE OF DENOMINATIONS (*continued*).

| No. | Stater. | Hecta. | Twelfth. | No. | Stater. | Hecta. | Twelfth. |
|---|---|---|---|---|---|---|---|
| 87 | × | | | 130 | × | × | |
| 88 | × | × | | 131 | × | | |
| 89 | × | | | 132 | × | | |
| 90 | × | × | | 133 | × | × | |
| 91 | × | × | | 134 | × | × | × |
| 92 | × | | | 135 | × | × | |
| 93 | × | × | | 136 | × | × | × |
| 94 | × | | | 137 | × | | |
| 95 | × | | | 138 | × | × | × |
| 96 | × | | | 139 | | × | |
| 97 | × | × | | 140 | × | × | |
| 98 | × | × | × | 141 | × | × | |
| 99 | × | × | | 142 | | | × |
| 99* | × | | | 143 | × | × | |
| 100 | × | × | × | 144 | × | | |
| 101 | | × | | 145 | | × | |
| 102 | × | × | | 146 | × | × | |
| 103 | × | | | 147 | | | |
| 104 | × | | | 148 | × | × | × |
| 105 | × | × | × | 149 | × | | |
| 106 | × | × | | 150 | | × | |
| 107 | × | × | × | 151 | × | | |
| 108 | × | × | | 152 | × | | |
| 109 | × | × | × | 153 | × | | |
| 110 | × | | | 154 | | × | × |
| 111 | | × | | 155 | × | | |
| 112 | | | × | 156 | | × | |
| 113 | × | × | | 157 | | × | × |
| 114 | | × | | 158 | × | × | |
| 115 | × | × | | 159 | | | × |
| 116 | | × | | 160 | | | × |
| 117 | × | | | 161 | × | | |
| 118 | × | | × | 162 | | × | |
| 119 | × | | | 163 | × | × | |
| 120 | × | × | | 164 | | × | |
| 121 | × | × | × | 165 | | | × |
| 122 | × | | | 166 | | | × |
| 123 | | × | | 167 | | × | |
| 124 | × | | | 168 | | × | × |
| 125 | × | | × | 169 | × | | |
| 126 | × | | | 170 | × | | |
| 127 | × | | | 171 | × | | |
| 128 | | × | × | 172 | × | | × |
| 129 | × | | | | | | |

## CATALOGUE OF TYPES.

1. *Obv.* Tunny upright between two pellets.

    *Rev.* Two incuse squares of different sizes; the larger one containing irregular forms, the other a cray-fish or scorpion.

    Brit. Mus., 252 grs. [Pl. I. 1].

    *Engr.* Num. Chron., N.S., vol. xv., Pl. X. 7. Brit. Mus. Guide, Pl. I., 12.

    *Noted.* Nummi Veteres, R. Payne Knight, p. 150.[30]

The tunny, here the principal type, assumes, as the symbol, badge, or "arms" of Cyzicus, its place on the earliest coinage of the state, a place it retained, though in a subordinate position, as long as Cyzicus continued to issue coins.

The incuse of the reverse is of a quite different form from that afterwards adopted and universally exhibited on the electrum coins of Cyzicus. The figure in one of the squares is probably a cray-fish (ἀστακός), a more likely adjunct on the money of a powerful maritime state than a scorpion. A similar creature occurs on coins once attributed to Abydos and later to Ancore, but now assigned by Dr. Imhoof-Blumer (Monnaies Grecques, p. 232) to Astakos.

This stater, of the Phocaic standard and of good weight, is the earliest coin which can be attributed to Cyzicus, and must be assigned to a period not much, if at all, later than the commencement of the sixth century B.C. It cannot, under any circumstances, be placed after the time when Crœsus introduced his gold coinage (B.C. 560), which, following in the track of his conquests, must to a

---

[30] In future this Catalogue will be cited as Num. Vet., R. P. K.

large extent have displaced the electrum money of the maritime cities of Asia Minor.

The tunny was a symbol of, and sacred to, Aphrodite-Astarte, but it is very doubtful if it is in connection with that goddess that it finds so important a place on the Cyzicene coinage. Except for the fact that all types on Greek money, and especially early ones, are sacred symbols, attached to some divinity, it might be supposed that the value of the fish as an article of trade was the reason why it was adopted as the badge of Cyzicus, in like manner as the silphium was in the Cyrenaica. It may, perhaps, be in a double capacity that both at Cyzicus and in the Cyrenaica these two important articles of commerce were adopted as state badges.

2. *Obv.* Male figure wearing himation over lower part of body, kneeling right on tunny; in his right hand he holds a long sceptre, and on his left an eagle, about to take flight.

*Rev.* Mill-sail incuse.[31]

Paris (De L.), 245·6 grs. [Pl. I. 2].

*Noted.* Ann. dell' Inst. di Corrisp. Archeol., xiii., p. 150*a*.

The figure is undoubtedly that of Zeus, though the kneeling position is one not quite consistent with a representation of the supreme god and father. He is identified by the eagle and sceptre, but in addition the whole figure is characteristic of the powers and attributes it was sought to idealise in a presentment of Zeus. Professor

---

[31] In the account of each type any description of the reverse will in future be omitted. It is invariably an incuse of the mill-sail pattern, and differs only in the quarters being sometimes plain, Pl. I., 1 A., at other times covered with dots, Pl. I., 1 B., or with short raised lines. The incuses which have dots or lines appear to be of the later issues.

Gardner (Types of Greek Coins, p. 87), regards the position as simply relative to the requirements of the composition on a limited space, an explanation which will also apply to others of the subjects found on the Cyzicene staters. Though a seated figure of Zeus would have equally well fitted the space at the artist's disposal, it is probable that the subject was in this case accommodated to suit the coin.

On a coin of Trajan is a figure of Zeus, with sceptre and eagle, and having an inscription, ZEY[Σ] ΣΩTHP KYZIKHNΩN.

    3. Bearded head to right, with ram's ear and horn. Beneath, tunny right.

        W. G. (*b*), 248 grs. [Pl. I. 3]. Brit. Mus. (*a*), 247·1. Paris (*c*), 247. Vienna, 247·2. Weber, 247·2 (Whittall sale, 1884, No. 743). Lambros (*a*).
        (*a*) same die, (*b*), (*c*), different dies.[32]

    *Engr.* Mionnet, Suppl. v., Pl. II. 3. Num. Chron., N.S. xvi., Pl. VIII. 10.

    *Noted.* Brandis, Das Münz-Mass- und Gewichtswesen, p. 408.

Mr. Head (Num. Chron. N.S., xvi., p. 280) believes the head to be of Dionysus Ammon rather than of Zeus Ammon, but there does not appear to be any sufficient reason to separate it from Zeus. On a coin of Macrinus, struck at Cyzicus, together with a laureate head, possibly of the Emperor, is one of Zeus-Ammon (Mionn., Suppl., v. p. 341, No. 385).

    4. Bearded head to left, laureate, with ram's ear and horn, hair hanging behind in three long curls. Beneath, tunny left.

---

[32] The letters (*b*) (*c*), &c., designate a die different from that noted (*a*), and also from each other.

Paris (De L.), (a), 247·6 grs. [Pl. I. 4]. St. Pet. (a) 246·8. W. G. (b), 245·2.
(a), same die, (b), diff. die.

*Engr.* Mém. de la Soc. Imp. d'Archéol. (1852), vi., Pl. XXI. 3.

*Noted.* Brandis, p. 408.

The head on this stater differs much in treatment from that on the last coin, and appears to be of an earlier date. Though the long flowing and curled hair is more in character with Dionysus than with Zeus, there do not appear to be any adequate grounds for attributing it to the former god.

5. Bearded head to left, wearing a wreath of marine plants; behind the neck the head of trident. Beneath, tunny left.

Berlin (Prokesch-Osten), 248·7 grs. [Pl. I. 5].

*Engr.* Revue Numis., N.S. ix., Pl. I. 7.

Hecta. Dupré sale (1869), No. 258.

As might be expected, Poseidon is likely to occur on the coinage of a great maritime state, and several staters will be found to contain the figure of the god, or, as in this case, his head, or some subject connected with him.

6. Bearded figure, kneeling on right knee to right, on tunny. On his extended right hand he holds a dolphin, and in his left a trident downwards. He wears a chlamys, ending in a tassel, which does not appear to pass round the neck, but over the left shoulder.

Brit. Mus., 247·4 grs. [Pl. I. 6]. One (248·7) noted Num. Chron., N.S., xvi., p. 281, No. 9.

*Engr.* Num. Chron., N.S., xvi., Pl. VIII. 12.

Poseidon is frequently represented on vases holding a dolphin, but on one (Lenormant and De Witte, Élite des Mon. Céram., iii., Pl. VIII), he holds a fish, possibly a tunny.

> 7. Bearded figure, wearing chlamys wrapped round left arm and flying behind, seated right on sea-horse, and striking with a trident, held in right hand. Beneath, tunny right.
>
> St. Pet., 247 grs. [Pl. I. 7]. This stater was found near Kertch.
>
> *Engr.* Ant. du Bosphore Cimmér., ii., p. 154. Wieseler, Denkmäler, ii., Pl. VII. 79.

Poseidon occurs twice on a cylix (671) in the Brit. Mus., wearing chlamys, riding on a sea-horse, and carrying a trident over his shoulder, in one case upwards, in the other downwards. (Lenormant and De Witte, Élite des Mon. Céram., iii., Pt. I., Pl. I. A, and Gerhard, Griech. Vasenbilder, Pl. VIII.

> 8. Bearded figure, half-draped, riding on dolphin, left, and holding a tunny by the tail in right hand.
>
> Paris (De L.), 40·2 grs. [Pl. I. 8].

Though without a trident or any other distinctive characteristic, the figure is probably Poseidon.

> 9. Youthful male figure, naked, riding on dolphin, left, and holding a tunny by the tail in right hand.
>
> W. G. (*a*), 245·2 grs., [Pl. I. 9]. Brit. Mus. (*b*), 247, (Thomas sale, No. 1777). Paris (*c*), 247.
> (*a*), (*b*), (*c*), diff. dies.
>
> *Engr.* Mém. de la Soc. Imp. d'Archéol, vi. Pl. XXI.
>
> *Noted.* Mionnet, Suppl., x. p. 228. No. 8. Brandis, p. 405.

The type, a figure of Taras, son of Poseidon, is almost identical with the well-known one of the Tarentine didrachms, from which it differs only in having the tunny in addition. This coin, like others of the staters and as that next to be described, is essentially a copy of a subject occurring on the money of another state.

10. Naked youth on horseback to left; his right arm is stretched out over the head of the horse, which he is about to crown. Beneath, tunny left.

St. Pet., 228·8 grs.[33] [Pl. I. 10].

*Engr.* Mém. de la Soc. Imp. d'Archéol., vol. vi. (1852), Pl. XXI. 6, described p. 370, No. 10.

Like the last described stater this is a direct copy of one of the common types of Tarentum; not a singular instance, as will be seen in the sequel, where types belonging to Gela, &c., are found on the staters.

11. Bearded human figure naked, the lower part ending in the tail of a fish, reclining in a fronting position, but to the left, on the right arm; the left hand is raised and holds a wreath or ring. Beneath, tunny left.

Brit. Mus. 246 grs. [Pl. I. 11].

*Engr.* Sestini, Stat. Ant., Pl. V. 15.

*Noted.* Num. Vet. R. P. K., p. 59. Mionnet, vol. vi., 616, No. 20.

Hecta. Carfrae (*a*), 41 grs. (Dundas sale, No. 21). [Pl. I. 12]. Berlin (two), (Prok.-Ost.), 41·3, another (plated), 31·5. W. G. (*b*), 41·9.
(*a*), (*b*), diff. dies.

*Engr.* Prokesch-Osten, Inéd. (1854), Pl. IV. 3.

*Noted.* Brandis, p. 406.

---

[33] Unless the weight is incorrectly given, this coin is probably plated.

The left hand on the stater is off the flan of the coin, but on the hecta in Mr. Carfrae's collection it distinctly holds a wreath or ring.

The subject is probably Triton, and corresponds to many representations of the son of Poseidon. It is difficult to explain what is held in the left hand, nor do other figures of Triton throw any light upon it.

On a coin wrongly attributed by Combe to Corcyra is a figure of Dagon much like this, holding a trident in his right hand with which he is striking, whilst the left holds up a round object (Museum Hunter., Pl. XIX., No. 12). Dagon is somewhat similarly represented, and holds what looks like a wreath, upon a coin of Aradus (Millingen, Sylloge, p. 81, Pl. IV. 61), and on a coin which M. Six (Num. Chron., N.S., vol. xviii. p. 125, Pl. VI. 3), is inclined to attribute to Azotus, he holds a trident in his right hand and a wreath in his left. On the coins of Itanus the figure which ends in a fish tail, and is not unlike that on the staters, is called by Mr. Wroth, though with a query, Glaucus. (Brit. Mus. Cat. of Cretan Coins, p. 51, Pl. XIII. 1, 2, 3).

12. Female head to left, wearing a veil with corn-wreath over it, the ears of corn projecting in front. Beneath, tunny left.

  Paris (De L.) (*a*), 246·9 grs., [Pl. I. 13]. Brit. Mus. (*b*), 247·4, (Thomas sale, No. 1778, Northwick, No. 958). Paris, 246·9.
  (*a*), (*b*), diff. dies.

  *Engr.* Rev. Num. N.S., vol. i. Pl. II. 9. Brit. Mus. Guide, Pl. XVIII. 7. Gardner, Types of Greek Coins, Pl. X. 41.

This beautiful head of Demeter belongs to the later

series of electrum coins of Cyzicus, and may, perhaps, be classed to the second quarter of the fourth century B.C.

The goddess has here the mature expression of the mother, with all the soft and gentle character of one so intimately connected with the productive gifts of nature. A somewhat similar but more youthful and virgin-like head of Cora, with the title ΣΩΤΕΙΡΑ, is found on the tetradrachms of Cyzicus. That the head is of Cora appears to be shown by a coin of Imperial times which has upon it a youthful head and the legend ΚΟΡΗ ΣΩ-ΤΕΙΡΑ ΚΥΖΙΚΗΝΩΝ.

> 13. Female head facing, but slightly inclining to left, with corn-leaves and ears wreathed in the hair, and wearing a veil and plain necklace. Beneath, tunny left.
> 
> Paris, 248·5 grs., [Pl. I. 14].
> 
> *Engr.* Head, Hist. Num., Fig. 272.

This head of Demeter, like that on the last described stater, belongs to the later series of the Cyzicenes. It was copied on coins of Tyra in Sarmatia, which have on the reverse a bull butting; also a type which occurs on the staters of Cyzicus.

> 14. Female figure, apparently half-length, to right, wearing long chiton, and holding in each hand a lighted torch, behind her a poppy. Beneath, tunny right.
> 
> Hirsch, 248 grs., [Pl. I. 15].
> 
> *Engr.* D'Alexéieff, Dissertation sur une monnaie inédite, Pl. Fig. 7. Paris, 1876.

The figure is Demeter, as is indicated by the torches and the poppy. The coin unfortunately is in poor condition, and it is, therefore, impossible to decide with certainty as to the attitude. She does not seem to be represented as standing, but rather as if sinking into the ground. If this supposition is correct, she appears as on her way in pursuit of Persephone to the lower world.

As Cyzicus was one of the places which claimed to be the scene of the rape of Persephone, it might be expected that Demeter would be represented on the coinage of the city.

15. Female figure, wearing long chiton and peplos, kneeling right on tunny; she holds a long torch (?) in her right hand.

   Paris (De L.), 245·2 grs. [Pl. I. 16]. St. Pet. 245·3.
   Both same die.

   *Engr.* Ant. de Bosph. Cimmér, vol. ii. p. 154. Rev. Num., N.S., vol. i., Pl. II. 8.

   *Noted.* Brandis, p. 407.

   The stater in the collection at the Hermitage was found near Kertch.

The object held in the right hand of the figure is doubtful. If, however, it is a torch, which appears probable, Demeter is represented.

16. Youthful figure right, wearing himation over the back, the breast and arms bare, holding two plants of corn in left hand, and carried in chariot drawn by two winged serpents. Beneath, tunny right.

   W. G. (*a*), 246·9 grs. [Pl. I. 17]. Brit. Mus. (*b*), 247·6. Paris (De L.), (*a*), 247. Carfrae (*a*), 246·3.
   (*a*), (*b*), diff. dies.

   *Engr.* Rev. Num., N.S. i., Pl. II. 7.

   *Noted.* Num. Vet., R. P. K., p. 31. Num. Chron., vi., p. 150. Brandis, p. 405.

There is no appearance of the chariot, though part of one wheel is visible beneath the wing of the serpent. This is, no doubt, due to the requirements of the coin. To have represented the chariot would have overcrowded the subject and detrimented the composition.

If the figure be female it is Demeter, and in the act of pursuing Hades when carrying off Persephone. The fullness of the breast is maternal, and the attitude, the right hand placed on the wing of the serpent, and the haste displayed, point to a mother's anxiety and her desire for the recovery of her child. Upon many of the Imperial coins of Cyzicus Demeter occurs, carried in a car drawn by serpents, and holding two torches.

The subject, however, with much more probability, represents Triptolemus starting on his beneficent mission, as the bestower of corn and fruits and the instructor of mankind in their cultivation. A very similar figure, though he there holds a sceptre, is shown on a cylix, figured in vol. iii. Pl. XLVI. of Lenormant and De Witte, Élite des Mon. Céram. The subject is not an uncommon one on vases.

The type, like others on the coins of Cyzicus, is probably due to the close relations between that state and Athens, where Demeter and the cycle connected with her were among the most ancient and intimate of its cults. A bronze coin of Eleusis—and there is a similar one of Athens—has a representation of Triptolemus quite like that of the stater, the car, however, being clearly shown. (Imhoof-Blumer, Monn. Grecq., p. 153, No. 101, Pl. C. No. 29. Overbeck, Griech. Kunst-Mythol., iii. p. 581; Münztafel, Pl. IX. No. 3).

17. Youthful male head, wearing laurel wreath, nearly full-face, but inclining to the right. Beneath, tunny right.

W. G. (*a*), 247·1 grs., [Pl. I. 18]. Brit. Mus. (*b*), 247·9. Paris (De L.), (*b*). Waddington, 246·8. Carfrae (*a*), 247·2 (Whittall sale, 1884, No. 789). Lambros in 1885.

(*a*), (*b*), diff. dies.

*Engr.* Waddington, Asie Mineure, Pl. VIII. 3. Rev. Num. xvii., Pl. V. 3. Num. Chron., N.S., xvi., Pl. VIII. 2.

A head of Apollo, who as the father of Cyzicus, the mythical founder of the city, and in other relations, was a favoured deity there.

18. Naked male figure, wearing wreath, kneeling right on tunny; his right arm hangs down his side, and in his left he holds a strung bow, and appears to be watching the effect of an arrow he has just discharged.

W. G. (*a*), 247·8 grs. (Bompois sale, No. 1372), [Pl. I. 19]. Brit. Mus. (*b*), 247·8. Berlin, 247.
   (*a*), (*b*), diff. dies.

*Engr.* Num. Chron., N.S., xvi., Pl. VIII. 4. Bompois Cat., Pl. V.

*Noted.* Königl. Münz-Kab. (1879), No. 100.

The figure of Apollo on the stater is probably copied from a group of which it formed a part. He is represented either as the destroyer of Python (as seen on a coin of Croton) or as shooting at the children of Niobe. The latter is the opinion of M. Six (Num. Chron., N.S., xvii., p. 170), who thinks the subject of Niobe and her children formed the central one on the front of a temple, and that kneeling figures of Apollo and Artemis occupied the two sides. He refers to a coin of Erchomenus in Arcadia (Num. Chron., N.S., xiii., Pl. V. 1), on which Artemis appears on one face and Niobe and one of her children on the other. By others the figures on the reverse are considered to be Callisto and Arcas.

A figure of Apollo, almost identical with that on the stater, occurs upon a small silver coin of Sicyon.

19. Figure wearing long chiton with sleeves, seated right on omphalos, holding a lyre in left hand; the right, which hangs down, holds an indefinite object, possibly a plectrum. Beneath, tunny right.

Berlin (Prok.-Ost.), 248·2 grs. [Pl. I. 20].

*Engr.* Rev. Num., N.S., ix., Pl. I. 8.

Though wearing a sleeved chiton, this is undoubtedly Apollo, to whom M. Lenormant attributes it (Rev. Num., N.S., ix., p. 13). There is no wreath apparent on the stater, but this may be due to imperfect striking. On a coin of Delphi the god is clothed in the same way. On silver coins of Cyzicus Apollo is represented on the omphalos, and holding a lyre, but naked to the waist, and wearing a wreath. On a half obol of Sicyon, Apollo, holding a lyre, is seated on what has been usually called a rock, but which is probably the omphalos. The type on the preceding stater also corresponds with that on another half obol of Sicyon.

20. Male figure, laureate, wearing peplos over knees, seated sideways, but with head turned to left, on griffin to right; in his right hand he holds a laurel bough. Beneath, tunny right.

Evans, 244·8 grs. [Pl. I. 21].

This stater was found near Kertch.

The Hyperborean Apollo, on his way to the country where the griffins had charge of the gold, of which Herodotus (iii. 116) gives an account. Although Apollo occurs on several of the Cyzicene electrum coins, and is very fully represented on the silver money of the state, such a subject as the present one was most appropriate, for it is certain that much of the gold used for the currency was obtained, through Panticapæum, from the Ural Mountains, the locality indicated by the griffin-guarded land of Apollo.

A similar subject, but where Apollo holds a lyre in the left hand, occurs on a cylix in the Imperial Museum at Vienna. (Lenormant and De Witte, Élite des Mon. Céram. vol. ii. Pl. V). The same is to be found on a coin of Trebonianus Gallus, struck at Alexandria Troas. (Mionnet, Suppl., vol. v. p. 541, No. 300). On a vase at Berlin Apollo is seated on a griffin, holding a laurel bough, but is clothed in a himation and wears buskins, as if equipped for a journey, probably to the Hyperborean regions (Lenormant and De Witte, l.c., vol. ii. Pl. XLIV). And on a vase in the Brit. Mus. (E. 694) he is represented on a griffin, laureate, and carrying a laurel bough, but only wearing peplos over his knees.

21. Figure seated sideways on swan, but with head turned to left, wearing peplos over knees. Beneath, tunny left.

Paris (De L.), 247 grs. [Pl. I. 22]. St. Pet., 250·5. Both same die.

*Engr.* Rev. de la Numis. Belg., vol. ii. Pl. V. 1.

*Noted.* Ant. du Bosph. Cimmér., vol. ii., p. 155. Brandis, p. 407.

The stater at the Hermitage was found near Kertch.

It is difficult to decide with certainty as to the sex of the figure. If female, it must be Aphrodite. On coins of Camarina, where a somewhat similar representation is found, the way in which the peplos is treated as a sail gives a more graceful character to the subject. The nymph Camarina, and not Aphrodite, is represented on the Sicilian coin.

The figure, however, is almost certainly male, and represents Apollo carried on a swan to Delos. Callimachus in his Hymn to Apollo says,

———ἐπένευσεν ὁ Δήλιος ἡδύ τι φοῖνιξ
Ἐξαπίνης ὁ δὲ κύκνος ἐν ἤερι καλὸν ἀείδει.

De Koehne (Ant. du Bosph. Cimmér., vol. ii. p. 155), referring to the stater found near Kertch, calls the figure Apollo, and attributes it to Chalcedon.

On a vase once in the Hamilton Collection, Apollo is represented wearing himation and buskins, seated on a swan, and holding a lyre. (Lenormant and De Witte, Élite des Mon. Céram. vol. ii., Pl. XLII).

The representation on a vase in the Brit. Mus. (E. 240), where Apollo is without a lyre, and holds a laurel bough, is more like that on the stater.

> 22. The Omphalos, with fillets suspended from the top; on each side is seated an eagle, with closed wings, the one facing the other. Beneath, tunny right.
>
> Imhoof (*a*), 245·8 grs. [Pl. I. 23]. Brit. Mus. (*a*), 248. Copenhagen. W. G. (*a*), 248·5. Bunbury. Weber, 247·5. Jones. Lewis. Six, 248·2. Rhousopoulos. Lambros.
> (*a*) same die.
>
> *Engr.* Num. Chron., N.S., xvi., Pl. VIII. 6. Brit. Mus. Guide, Pl. X. 12. Bompois Cat., Pl. V.

The Omphalos at Delphi, where was situated the great oracle of Apollo. The representation here probably alludes, as Mr. Head suggests (Num. Chron., N.S., xvi., p. 279), to the worship of the god in general, and as typical of the Apolline cult throughout Hellas. At the same time Cyzicus had, through its reputed founder, a very intimate connection with Apollo.

The golden eagles of Zeus at Delphi are mentioned by Pindar (Pyth., iv. 4) in reference to the oracle,

ἔνθα ποτὲ χρυσέων Διὸς ἀιητῶν πάρεδρος.

The scholiasts connect these images with the legend that Zeus sent forth one eagle from the east and another from the west to find the centre of the world, and that they met at the oracle of Delphi.

23. Helios, naked, radiate, kneeling right on tunny, holding by the bridle two horses, prancing in opposite directions.

W. G. (*a*), 247·8 grs. [Pl. I. 24]. Brit. Mus. (*b*), 248·4. Berlin, 247·4. Weber, 247·3. Hirsch (*c*), 247. Lambros in 1885.
(*a*), (*b*), (*c*), diff. dies.

*Engr.* Num. Chron., N.S., xvi., Pl. VIII. 5. Gardner, Types, Pl. X. 3.

Hecta. Brit. Mus., 40·2 grs.

*Noted.* Brandis, p. 407.

The Sun God appears on the stater radiate, as on coins of Rhodes. He was worshipped at Zeleia, a town on the river Aesepus, and neighbouring to Cyzicus, as Helios (Marquardt, Cyzicus und sein Gebiet, p. 129), and probably also at Cyzicus itself.

The subject, as here represented, is very gracefully composed, and has probably, as is suggested by M. Six (Num. Chron., N.S. xvii., p. 170), been copied from a metope of a temple. He observes, "La composition est parfaitement carrée." It has, however, been accommodated to suit the requirements of the size and shape of the coin flan, a mode of procedure not uncommon with the artist die-engravers of Cyzicus.

Representations of Helios with the chariot are not infrequent upon vases (Lenormant and De Witte, Élite des Mon. Céram., vol. ii. Pl. CXI., CXII.A., CXIII.).

24. Young male head to left, with stag's horn. Beneath, tunny left.

    Athens (*a*), 247·9 grs. [Pl. I. 25]. W. G. (*a*), 246·8 (Whittall sale, 1884, No. 747), [Pl. I. 26]. Brit. Mus. (*b*), 247·1.
        (*a*), (*b*), diff. dies.

*Engr.* Num. Chron., N.S. xvi., Pl. VIII. 19.
*Noted.* Num. Vet., R. P. K. p. 126.

The head of Actæon, and connected with the worship of Artemis. It is the only coin subject having relation to the goddess which has up to the present time been found on the staters, though she was worshipped in a temple not far from Cyzicus, at a place where there were hot springs. This seems to be the only instance where Actæon is represented upon a Greek coin. He appears on vases as a youth, with stag's horns sprouting from his forehead, and being attacked by his dogs (Lenormant and De Witte, Élite des Mon. Céram., vol. ii. Pl. C, CI, CIII).

25. Female head to left, wearing crested helmet with cheekpieces; the socket for the crest is ornamented with a zigzag pattern and dots, similar to that on the early tetradrachms of Athens. The hair, which hangs down beneath the back of the helmet, is represented by dots. Beneath, tunny left.

    W. G. (*a*), 248·2 grs. (Bompois sale, No. 1369), [Pl. II. 1]. Brit. Mus. (*a*), 247. Weber (*a*), 246·5. Imhoof (*a*), 249·9. Hoffmann, 247·4.
        (*a*) same die.

*Engr.* Imhoof-Blumer, Choix, Pl. III, 99. Head, Hist. Num. Fig. 271.
*Noted.* Imhoof-Blumer, Monn. Grecq., p. 241, No. 67.

Hecta. Brit. Mus. (*a*), 40·8 grs. Vienna (two), 40 (*b*), 42·6. Berlin (*c*), 40·6. Athens, 41·2. W. G. (*d*), 41·4.
        (*a*), (*b*), (*c*), (*d*), diff. dies.

Twelfth. Paris (De L.).
*Engr.* De Luynes, Choix, Pl. X, 13.

The head of Pallas is a type which occurs at various periods on the Cyzicene staters. This coin is archaic, and is probably not later than B.C. 500; others belong to a time when Greek art was at its height. It is possible that in these representations a part of the goddess may stand for the whole, and that the head is intended for Pallas herself. If this supposition is true we may have here one portion of a group, other parts of which are found on other coins, as, for instance, in the subject of Gaia, Erichthonius, and Cecrops, in which Pallas was a principal actor. A coin of Agrigentum, which has on one face the head of an eagle, and on the other a crab's claw, affords a good example where part of a type is put for the whole.

That Pallas, the goddess of Athens, should occupy a prominent place in the coinage of Cyzicus, is only what might be expected when the long and intimate relationship between the two states is taken into consideration. Several types having reference to Athens will be found to occur on the staters.

26. Female head to left, wearing a plain Corinthian helmet, the hair behind hanging in a square mass, and represented by dots. Behind, tunny downwards.

Imhoof (*a*), 248·7 grs. [Pl. II. 2]. Brit. Mus., 249·6. Vienna (*b*), 239·3. Weber (*c*), 249·1. W. G. (*c*), 248·2. Lambros in 1885.

(*a*), (*b*), (*c*), diff. dies.

Hecta. Munich, 40·8 grs. The Hague.

*Engr.* Sestini, Stat. Ant., Pl. VI. 15.

*Noted.* Mionnet, Suppl. v., p. 370, No. 549.

An archaic coin, and probably a head of Pallas.

27. Female head to left, wearing crested helmet. Behind, tunny upwards.

St. Pet., 246·9 grs. [Pl. II. 3].

Hecta. Six, 41 grs. [Pl. II. 4].

Both the stater and hecta are in very poor condition, and it is therefore difficult to make out the form of the helmet. The head is probably of Pallas.

28. Female head to left, wearing crested Corinthian helmet, hair in a long roll behind. Beneath, tunny left.

Paris (De L.) (*a*), 247 grs. [Pl. II. 5]. Brit. Mus. (*b*), 246·8 (Thomas sale, No. 1779; Loscomb sale, No. 575). Berlin (Fox), 246·9. St. Pet. (two), 247·2 (*c*), 247·3 (*d*).

(*a*), (*b*), (*c*), (*d*), diff. dies.

*Engr.* Mém. de la Soc. Imp. d'Archéol, vol. vi., Pl. XXI. 4. Fox, Unpubl. Coins, II., No. 25.

*Noted.* Brandis, p. 409.

Again a head of Pallas.

29. Female head, nearly full face, but inclining to right, wearing helmet with three crests. Beneath, tunny right.

Paris (De L.) (*a*), 247·2 grs. [Pl. II. 6]. Berlin (*b*), 247. Athens (*b*), 248·1. W. G. (*a*), 247·1. Weber (*b*), 245·9. (Bompois sale, No. 1370).

(*a*), (*b*), diff. dies.

*Noted.* Königl. Münz-Kab., 1877, No. 99.

Still a head of Pallas.

30. Beardless head, full-faced, without neck, wearing a helmet with a crest which has the appearance of an inverted crescent, with a row of dots upon the lower part of crest. Beneath, tunny left.

W. G. (*a*), 245·1 grs. (Whittall sale, 1884, No. 756), [Pl. II. 7]. Paris (*b*), 247.

(*a*), (*b*), diff. dies.

*Engr.* Mionnet, Suppl., v. p. 301. No. 109, Pl. II. 5.

*Noted.* Brandis, p. 408.

The crescent-like object upon the head appears to be the crest of a helmet, and the line of dots favours that view. The head, without any neck and with peculiar projecting ears, scarcely appears like that of Pallas, and is somewhat Gorgon-like. It possibly may be a Gorgon head, and wearing, in connection with Pallas, the helmet of that goddess. The way in which the crest is represented may be the result of an inability to show it in perspective, for such a representation would require the face to be turned a little on one side. A parallel instance is found in the way in which the eye is placed, as if seen in front, upon a face seen in profile.

31. Female figure to right, wearing sleeveless chiton; she is rising through the ground, and holds in her outstretched arms a child, as if presenting it to someone. The child is naked, except that it wears a belt, with bullæ attached, which passes over the left shoulder and under the right arm. Beneath, tunny right.

W. G., 247·5 grs. (Bompois sale, No. 1378), [Pl. II. 8].
Brit. Mus., 247·5. (Whittall sale, 1884, No. 755).
Both same die.

*Engr.* Head, Hist. Num. Fig. 277.

The representation is of Gaia giving Erichthonius into the hands of Athena, and is a portion of a group, the original of which was probably in marble. The figure of Cecrops on the stater next to be described formed another portion of the subject, to complete which Athena is wanting. No coin has yet come to light which gives the figure of the goddess, but there probably was one, unless she is represented by a coin bearing her head, as already suggested. The group from which the subjects of these two staters were taken, must have borne a strong likeness to a terra-cotta at Berlin (Archæol. Zeitung, 1872, p. 51, Pl.

LXIII), and though there are some slight variations, it is probable that the terra-cotta and the prototype of the staters were both copied from a common and well-known piece of Attic sculpture.

The crepundia which Erichthonius wears may be seen on the alliance coins of Samos, Ephesus, &c., which have the type of Heracles strangling the serpents, and also on a gold stater of Lampsacus.

The subject is found upon vases. See Lenormant and De Witte, Élite des Mon. Céram., vol. i. Pl. LXXXIV., LXXXV. On a hydria in the British Museum (E. 197), the birth of Erichthonius is represented, the figures there being a nymph, Zeus, Gaia holding the child, Athena, and Nike.

32. Bearded figure to left, the body ending in a serpent's tail; in his right hand he holds a branch of a tree, upright. Beneath, tunny left.

Imhoof (*a*), 248·7 grs. [Pl. II. 9]. Brit. Mus. (*b*), 246·8, [Pl. II. 10]. Berlin, 247·6. St. Pet. (*a*), 247·7. W. G. (*a*), 248·1. (Whittall sale, 1884, No. 744). Jones. Lambros, 249.
(*a*), (*b*), diff. dies.

*Engr.* Num. Chron., N.S., xvi., Pl. VIII. 14, 15. Zeitschr. für Numis., vi. p. 16 (woodcut). Brit. Mus. Guide, Pl. X. 14. Gardner, Types, Pl. X. 1.

Hecta. Paris.

Mr. Head (Num. Chron., N.S., xvi., p. 281) attributed the figure to one of the giants of Mount Dindymus, who attacked the ships when the Argonauts had ascended the mountain. There is no doubt, however, as M. Six has suggested in a letter to Mr. Head, printed l. c. xvii. p. 169, that it represents Cecrops, and is part of a group where Gaia is presenting Erichthonius to Athena. The serpent, in allusion to his autochthonous, earth-born origin, is a frequent adjunct of Cecrops, and in the present instance forms a portion of his body:—

ὦ Κέκροψ ἥρως ἄναξ, τὰ πρὸς ποδῶν δρακοντίδη. Aristoph. Vesp., 438.

The branch he holds is from the olive-tree on the hill of the Acropolis, planted by Athena, and by which she established her right to the country in the dispute with Poseidon.

Cecrops is represented ending in a serpent's tail and holding an olive-branch, on a vase. (Lenormant and De Witte, Élite des Mon. Céram., vol. i. Pl. LXXXV. A.).

A very similar treatment to that in the group from which the type of this and the preceding coin seem to have been taken, is found on a crater (Mon. Ined. dell' Inst., vol. iii. Pl. XXX). Hephæstus is, however, present. On a cylix (l. c. vol. x. Pl. XXXIX), there is a group somewhat like the last, but where, in addition to Hephæstus, Herse also is present. On both of these vases Cecrops is represented ending in a serpent's tail. A rhyton in the British Museum (E. 471), has a figure of Cecrops with a serpent's tail, and holding a sceptre and a patera, into which a winged figure is about to pour a libation. Erichthonius, who is seated on a rock, appears as a youth wrapped in a mantle.

33. Female head to left, wearing stephane and earring. Beneath, tunny left.
Paris (a), 245·5 grs. [Pl. II. 11]. Brit. Mus. (b), 246·3, (Thomas sale, No. 1777). St. Pet. (b), 245·5.
(a), (b), diff. dies.
*Engr.* Brit. Mus. Guide, Pl. XVIII. 6.
*Noted.* Brandis, p. 408.

Probably a head of Aphrodite, and one of the later staters of Cyzicus, not earlier perhaps than the second quarter of the fourth century B.C.

34. Female figure standing facing, but inclining to left; she is naked to the waist, and holds up her dress with her right hand, the left apparently resting on a column, in front of which stands a naked youthful winged figure facing, the right arm raised and the legs crossed. Beneath, tunny left.

Paris, 247 grs. [Pl. II. 12].
*Noted.* Brandis, p. 407.

Aphrodite and Eros. The composition is one of great gracefulness, and is very skilfully balanced. The pose of the figures and their varied and appropriate attitudes are rendered in a very charming way. It was probably copied from a larger group in marble, a work of celebrity and by a great sculptor.

35. Head of Hermes to left, wearing petasus. Beneath, tunny left.

Waddington, 245·7 grs. (Ivanoff sale, No. 190).

This is almost the only type on a stater or its parts that I am acquainted with, of which I am unable to give a representation.

No other coin of Cyzicus bearing a subject connected with Hermes is known to me, unless those with a goat or goat's head may be considered as belonging to his cult.

36. Bearded head to right, wearing diadem (the mitra), and having an ivy wreath above and beneath it. Beneath, tunny right.

W. G. (*a*), 246·2 grs. (Bompois sale, No. 1367), [Pl. II. 13]. Brit. Mus. (*b*), 244·7. Paris (*a*), 246·3. One engraved Num. Chron., N.S. Pl. VIII. 8 (*a*), 246·2.
(*a*), (*b*), diff. dies.

*Engr.* Num. Chron., N.S., xvi., Pl. VIII. 7, 8.
*Noted.* Brandis, p. 408.

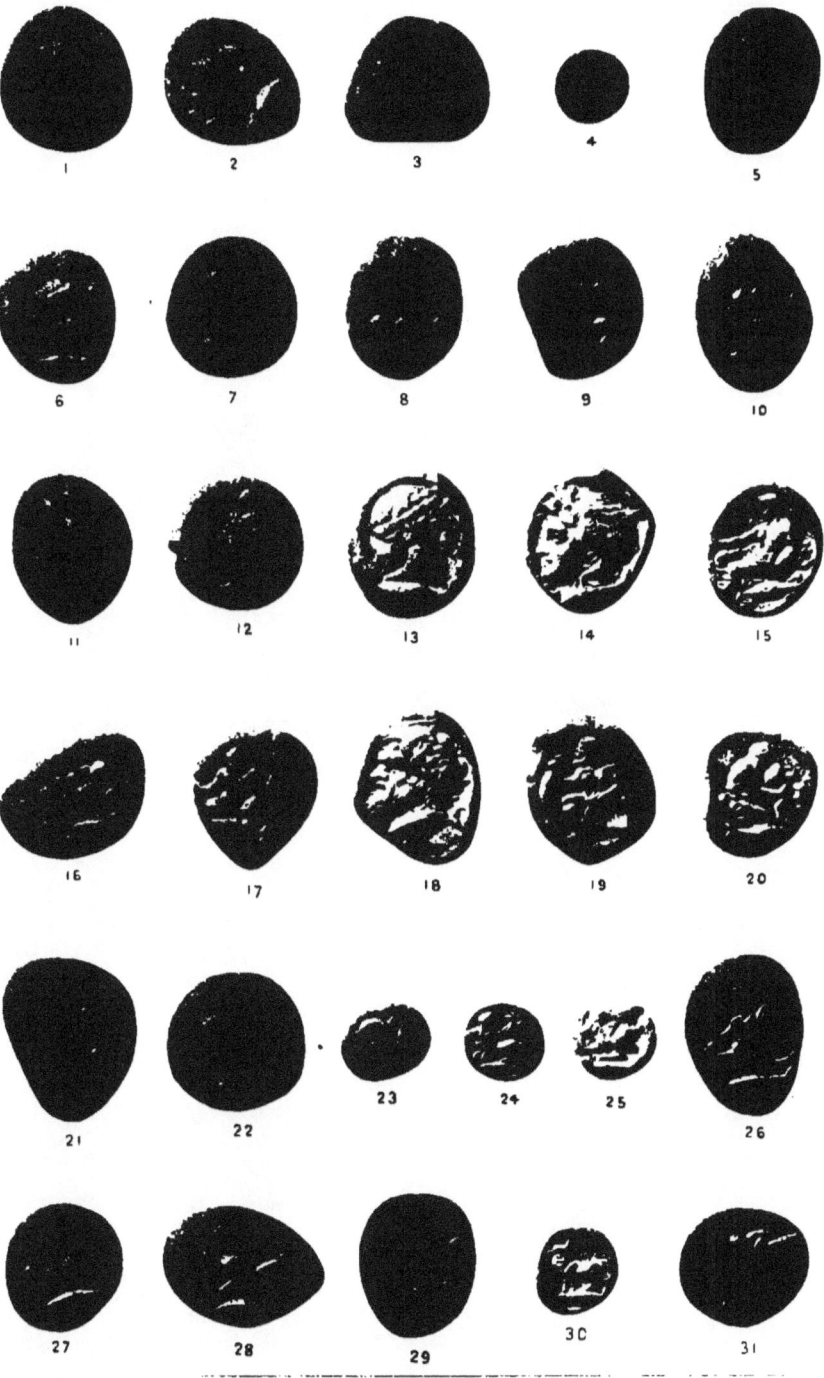

Head of Dionysus, as noble in expression as it is beautifully executed. The god is here presented as manifesting the strength and repose of nature, not as when she appears in the activity and tumult of production, but when she has provided all that sustains and gladdens the life of man, and rests, though without fatigue, from her labour.

It may be contrasted, and much to its advantage, with the head of the god on the coins of the Sicilian Naxus, which, beautiful as it is, does not possess the calm dignity of the Cyzicene picture. It may be compared with the head on the tetradrachms and drachms of Thasus, which for breadth of treatment and majestic quietness with strength, is not surpassed by any head in the whole Greek coin series.

37. Youthful head to left, wearing ivy wreath, with bunches of berries in front; hair long and flowing. Beneath, tunny left.

Imhoof (*a*), 248·6 grs. [Pl. II. 14]. Paris (*b*), 247·7. Berlin (two), (Prok.-Ost.) (*a*), 247·8, (Fox), 247·6.

(*a*), (*b*), diff. dies.

*Engr.* Rev. Num., N.S. ix., Pl. I. 5.

*Noted.* Brandis, p. 408. Königl. Münz-Kab. (1877), No. 106.

The head is very feminine, and though probably of young Dionysus, may be of a Dionysiac female, a Mænad.

38. Youthful male figure, wearing himation over the knees, and fillet, the ends of which hang low and are seen in front of and behind the head. He is seated left on a rock, which is covered with a panther's skin, the paws being visible beneath the tunny. He holds a cantharus in his right hand, and his left arm rests on the rock behind him. The head of the thyrsus, with pine-cone and tænia, projects in front of his knees. Beneath, tunny left.

Paris (De L.) (*a*), 247 grs. [Pl. II. 15]. Brit. Mus. (*b*), 245·2, [Pl. II. 16]. Paris (*a*), 246·2. Berlin (two), 245·8, 244·7. St. Pet., 247. Bunbury (Whittall sale, 1869, No. 39). Imhoof (*c*), 247.

(*a*), (*b*), (*c*), diff. dies.

*Engr.* Brit. Mus. Guide, Pl. XVIII. 5.

*Noted.* Brandis, p. 406. Königl. Münz-Kab. (1877), No. 102.

Hecta. Six, 39 grs.

*Engr.* Dumersan, Cat. Allier, Pl. XII. 5.

*Noted.* Mionnet, Suppl., v. p. 303, No. 121.

Dionysus is here figured youthful and beardless. He reclines in an attitude almost of languor, with limbs softly though fully moulded, and with even a feminine character, not inconsistent with the dimorphic attributes of the god. The panther's skin, the thyrsus and wine-cup, all fit in with the richly developed form, and are in closest harmony with the divinity in whom the wealth of a bounteous and genial nature was most fully expressed.

The coin is probably a copy from a sculpture on the pediment of a temple, and reminds us of the Heracles of Croton, which strikingly recalls the pedimental Theseus (so-called) of the Parthenon.

89. Youthful figure, naked, seated facing on tunny left; he wears a wreath of ivy and holds the thyrsus with pine-cone head and tænia in his left hand; the right hand is off the coin, but it possibly held a cantharus.

Paris, 248·5 grs. [Pl. II. 17].

Dionysus appears here as a child, almost an infant, but the nascent power of the god is shown in the firm pose of the figure and the decision with which he grasps the thyrsus.

40. Bearded head to left, with animal ears, and wreathed with ivy. Beneath, tunny left.

Berlin (Prok.-Ost.), 247·6 grs. [Pl. II. 18].
*Engr.* Rev. Num., N.S. ix., Pl. I. 3.
*Noted.* Königl. Münz-Kab. (1877), No. 107.

The head is of Pan, and but for the difference in the form of the leaves of the wreath, is almost identical with that on some of the gold coins of Panticapæum. The head of a member of the Dionysiac cycle would fitly appear on the coins of Cyzicus, but in addition, on account of the constant commercial relations between the two cities, the principal divinity of Panticapæum found a very appropriate place on a Cyzicene stater.

41. Bearded satyr with pointed ears and long and thick tail, kneeling to left, holds a tunny by the tail in his right hand, the left rests on his hip; hair represented by dots.

Imhoof (*a*), 248·6 grs. [Pl. II. 19]. Vienna (*b*), 247·4. W. G. (*b*), 249. Weber (*b*), 248·8. Hirsch (*b*), 247.
(*a*), (*b*), diff. dies.
*Engr.* Head, Hist. Num. Fig. 275.
Hecta. Paris (two), (De L.), 41·6 grs., 41·3. Leake, 41·4.
*Noted.* Leake, Num. Hell. Suppl. p. 44.

One of the earlier staters. Satyrs, as part of the Dionysiac cycle, might be expected to occur on coins of Cyzicus, and we shall accordingly find them on the staters under several different aspects. The characteristic features and form of these ignoble attendants upon Dionysus are well represented on the present coin, in the coarse and fleshy nose and lips, as well as in the strongly formed but ungraceful limbs.

42. Bearded satyr, with tail and animal ears, kneeling to right on tunny; he holds a cantharus in his right hand into which he is pouring wine from an amphora, held on his left arm.

> W. G. (*a*), 247·8 grs. [Pl. II. 20]. Brit. Mus. (*b*), 248. St. Pet., 245·7. Waddington, 246·7. Weber, 247·1. (Bompois sale, No. 1374). Carfrae, 247·8. Hoffmann. Lambros.
>
> (*a*), (*b*), diff. dies.
>
> *Engr.* Num. Chron., N.S. xvi., Pl. VIII. 9, vol. xx. Pl. I. 8. Head, Hist. Num. Fig. 274.

A subject which, with many others, belongs to the cycle of Dionysus, who himself is more than once depicted on the staters. Mr. Head (Num. Chron., N.S. xvi., p. 280) reminds us that Cyzicus was renowned for its wines, and quotes the line,

Κύζικ' ὦ δικήτειρα Προποντίδος οἰνοπόλοιο.

43. Satyr, with tail and animal ears, kneeling left on tunny, is drinking from an amphora which he holds up to his mouth with both hands; a wavy line depends from the amphora.

> W. G. 247·1 grs. [Pl. II. 21]. Collection at Athens. Both found at the Piræus with others in 1882, and both from the same die.

The amphora has the appearance of being broken at the neck, and certainly there is not room for it between the body of the vessel and the lips of the satyr. Such a representation would be a most unusual, not to say unlikely one; but it seems as if, in his eagerness to get the sooner at the wine, the satyr had broken off the mouth of the amphora. If this supposition can be entertained, the waved line may be a stream of wine escaping the lips of the too greedy drinker. On many vases where wine is being poured into a vessel and is being spilt in the operation or overflows, the appearance is much like that on the stater.

> 44. Bearded satyr seated right, holding a flute (?) in each hand. Beneath, tunny right.
> Brit. Mus. 247·9 grs. [Pl. II. 22]. Waddington, 247·2.
> *Engr.* Num. Chron., N.S. xvi., Pl. VIII. 20.

The object held in the satyr's left hand has also been supposed to be an idol.

> 45. Satyric mask, tongue protruding. On either side, a tunny upwards.
> Paris, 41 grs. [Pl. II. 23]. W. G., 41·1.
> Different dies.
> *Engr.* Mionnet, Suppl., vol. ix., p. 228, No. 7. Pl. X. 3.
> Twelfth. Munich, 20·5 grs.
> *Engr.* Sestini, Stat. Ant. Pl. VI. 18.
> *Noted.* Mionnet, vi. p. 620, No. 52. Suppl. v. p. 370, No. 551.

> 46. Centaur galloping left, with head turned back, holding a branch with both hands. Beneath, tunny left.
> Paris (*a*), 40·7 grs. [Pl. II. 24]. Munich (*a*), 41. Hague. St. Pet. (*a*). Imhoof (*b*), 39·8. Six (*c*), 35·8. (*a*), (*b*), (*c*), diff. dies.
> *Engr.* Sestini, Stat. Ant., Pl. V. 17, 18. Mionnet, Pl. XLIII. 9. Dumersan, Cat. Allier, Pl. XII. 4.

Centaurs formed a part of the Dionysiac cycle; but as represented here, armed and in conflict, probably with the Lapithæ, some other connection may perhaps be looked for, and possibly in association with Heracles. Another motive may, however, be suggested. Jason was brought up by the Centaur Cheiron, and this type may originate, like others, in the Argonautic expedition.

47. Bifrontal head, male to right, female to left. Beneath, tunny.

W. G., 40·9 grs. [Pl. II. 25]. St. Pet., 41·4.
Diff. dies.

The heads are those of a Satyr and Nymph. In the Inst. di Corr. Arch. Annali, 1858, Tav. d' Agg., is published a bifrontal vase, with heads of a Satyr and Nymph, back to back, with a memoir by De Witte.

48. Female figure, wearing long chiton, seated left on dolphin; she holds a wreath in her right hand, and carries a shield with a star upon it on her left arm. Beneath, tunny left.

W. G. (a), 247·4 grs. (Whittall sale, 1884, No. 749), [Pl. II. 26]. Weber (a), 248·7 (sale at Sotheby and Wilkinson's, Feb. 19, 1877, No. 78), [Pl. II. 27]. Brit. Mus. (a), 247·6 (Thomas sale, No. 1775). Paris (b), 247·6. Hoffmann (a), 247·0. Lambros in 1885.
(a), (b), diff. dies.

*Engr.* Mém. de la Soc. Imp. d'Archéol., vol. vi. (1852), Pl. XXI. 5. Num. Chron., N.S., xvi., Pl. VIII. 22. Brit. Mus. Guide, Pl. XVIII. 4.

M. de Koehne (l. c., p. 376), who first published the stater, considers the figure to be of Thetis, carrying the shield forged by Hephæstus and a wreath to Achilles, the vanquisher of Hector. It is more probable that it represents a Nereid, and that the coin was struck after a naval victory. The date, judging by the style and fabric, may well be about B.C. 410, and it quite possibly may have commemorated the victory gained by the Athenians under Alcibiades over the Spartan fleet, off Cyzicus, in that year, at which time the city was under Athenian hegemony. Upon a stater of Lampsacus, in the collection in the Bibliothèque, Paris, is a very similar figure, though having some slight variations. (Sestini, Stat. Ant., Pl. VI. 13.)

49. Female figure, naked, to left, her hair tied in a knot at the back of head; two dogs' heads issue from her shoulder, and she ends in the tail of a fish; in her right hand she holds a tunny. Beneath, tunny left.

St. Pet., 246·9 grs. [Pl. II. 28].

*Engr.* Mém. de la Soc. Imp. d'Archéol., vol. vi., Pl. XXI. 7.

Scylla, and as usually represented. This type is only found elsewhere upon coins of Italy and Sicily, and then merely as an ornament or adjunct, except on a coin of Cumæ. A celebrated Cyzicene painter, Androcydes, a rival of Zeuxis, was known for having produced as one of his best works a picture of Scylla.

50. Bearded human-headed bull, with horns, face fronting, standing left on tunny.

Athens, 245 grs. [Pl. II. 29].

Hecta. Munich, 40·9 grs. [Pl. II. 30].

Twelfth. Athens, 20 grs.

The symbolic representation of a river-god, and possibly of the river Aesepus.

51. Forepart of human-headed bull, with beard and horns, swimming to right. Behind, tunny upwards.

Brit. Mus. (*a*), 246·5 grs. [Pl. II. 31]. Paris (*b*). Berlin (Fox), 247·4. W. G. (*a*), 247 grs. (Whittall sale, 1884, No. 748). Leake, 247·4.

(*a*), (*b*), diff. dies.

> *Engr.* Rev. de la Numis. Belg., ii. Pl. V. 2. Num. Chron., N.S., xvi., Pl. VIII. 21. Brit. Mus. Guide, Pl. X. 10. Zeit. für Numis., vol. ii. p. 123 (woodcut).
>
> *Noted.* Leake, Num. Hellen. Suppl., p. 44.
>
> Hecta. Brit. Mus., 41 grs.

This type is identical with that so frequent on the coins of Gela, and Von Sallet (Zeit. für Num., vol. ii. p. 123) considers that it is merely a copy of those coins. Mr. Head (Num. Chron., N.S., xvi. p. 283) inclines to believe it represents either the river Aesepus or the Rhyndacus, both in Cyzicene territory. I prefer Von Sallet's explanation, nor can I see anything in the subject specially connected with Cyzicus. Many of the staters contain direct reproductions of the types of other cities, and the practice was not infrequent with the Cyzicene mint.

> 52. Winged female figure, wearing peplos over knees, kneeling to left, and holding an aplustre in the right hand in front of her face; her left arm, which is wrapped in the peplos, rests on her hips. Beneath, tunny left.
>
> Paris (*a*), 247 grs. [Pl. III. 1]. Brit. Mus. (*a*), 245·4. W. G. (*a*), 245·7. (Bompois sale, No. 1377). Carfrae, 246·6. R. and F.
> (*a*) same die.
>
> *Engr.* Rev. Num., N.S., vol. i., Pl. II. 5. Gardner, Types, Pl. X. 2.
>
> *Noted.* Num. Chron. vi. p. 151. Leake, Num. Hellen. Suppl. p. 44.
>
> Hecta. St. Pet., 41 grs.

The figure is of Nike, and, as she holds an aplustre, the victory commemorated must have been a naval one. It may, as in the case of the stater No. 48, have been struck

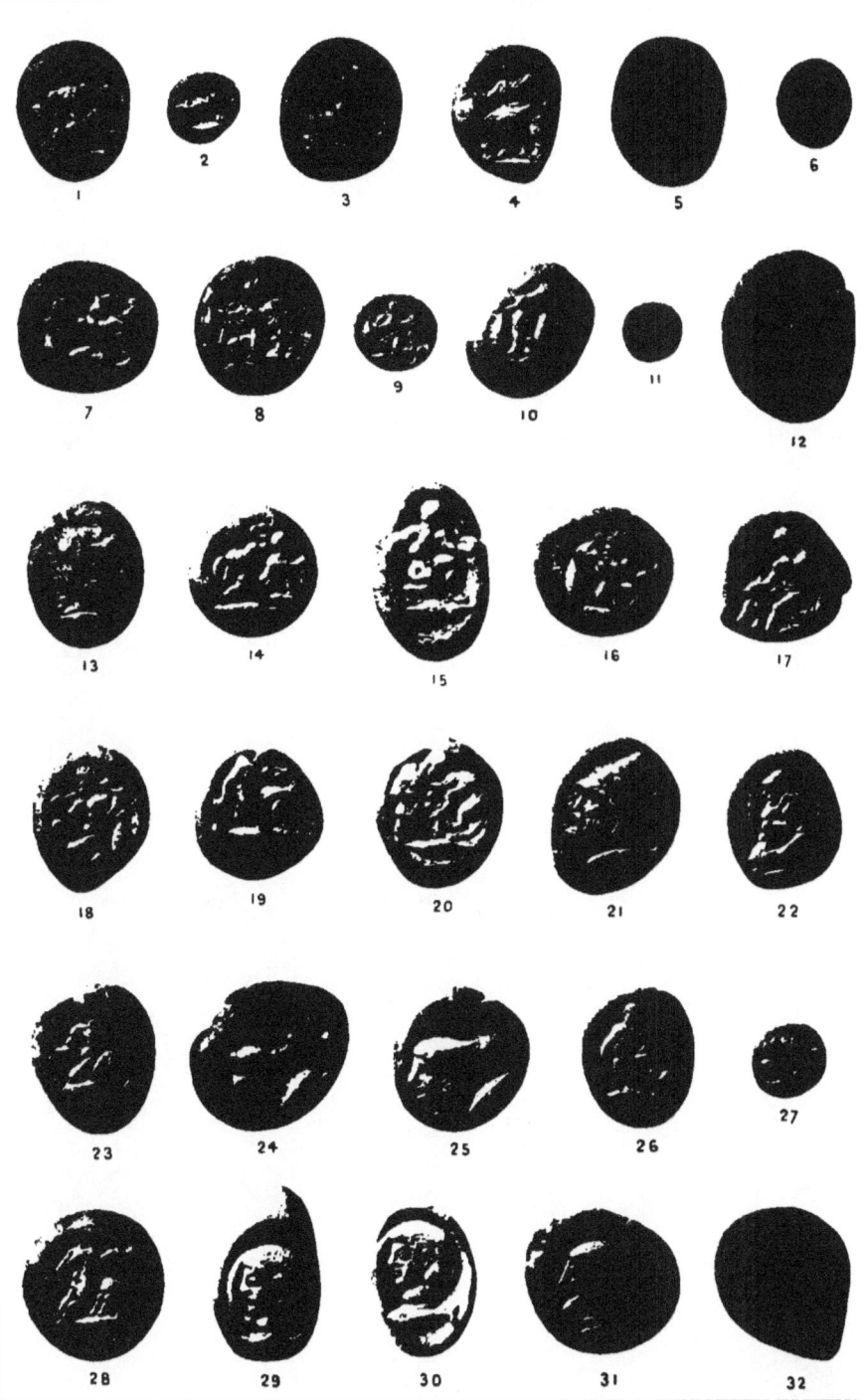

CYZICUS.

after the battle off Cyzicus, B.C. 410. If this be so, we have two coins serving as a memorial of the same event. This, however, need cause no difficulty, and it is not improbable that the two staters may have been issued in different years and under the authority of different magistrates, which would naturally cause a change in the treatment of the memorial-type. Indeed, if we may judge by its art and other characteristics, the die for this stater may have been engraved a few years after that of No. 48, which would account for the slight advance in style which it appears to exhibit. At the time in question art was developing with great rapidity, and was about to culminate at the highest point it has ever reached, when a short period was sufficient to allow of a material change in design, fabric, and workmanship. M. Charles Lenormant (Rev. Num., N.S., vol. i. p. 38, *note*) supposes the stater to have been struck in commemoration of the victory of Timotheus over the Peloponnesian fleet, B.C. 375, which he considers was a deliverance for Cyzicus. There can be no doubt, as I have stated above, that the type was connected with a naval victory, but not one so late as that suggested. Nor does the victory in question appear to be one sufficiently important to Cyzicus to have induced her to commemorate it on her coinage.

This is perhaps the first instance where Nike appears on a coin as the goddess of victory in war. On the coins of other Greek states she seems to be, up to this date and onwards, until the time of Alexander and the Diadochi, the goddess of agonistic victory. The only representation of the same import with which we are acquainted is the well-known tetradrachm of Demetrius Poliorcetes, where Victory stands on a prow blowing a trumpet.

53. Winged female figure, wearing long chiton, flying to right, with outstretched hands, and holding a wreath. In front, tunny upwards.

Hecta. Berlin, 40·7 grs. [Pl. III. 2].

Again a figure of Nike.

54. Female figure, wearing long chiton and peplos, seated left, holds a wreath in her right hand, her left resting on the seat behind her, upon which is inscribed ΕΛΕΥ ΟΕΡΙ. Beneath, tunny left.

Paris, 246·1 grs. [Pl. III. 3]. St. Pet., 248. Found near Kertch.
Both same die.
*Engr.* Millingen, Anc. Coins, Pl. V. 18. Mionnet, Suppl., v. p. 304, No. 127, Pl. III. 3. Ant. du Bosph. Cimmér, vol. ii. p. 154. Mon. Ined. dell' Inst., vol. i. Pl. LVII. B. 4.

*Noted.* Brandis, p. 407.

Twelfth. Löbbecke, 19·4. It is inscribed ΕΛ [Ε]Υ

*Noted.* Zeit für Numis., xii. p. 312.

The figure is no doubt one of Eleutheria.

This stater appears to be of a later date than Nos. 48 and 52, and may be attributed to the commencement of the fourth century B.C. The victory of Conon over the Lacedæmonian fleet under Peisander, near Cnidus, in B C. 394, had put an end to the Spartan rule in Asia, which had existed since the battle of Ægospotami, opposite Lampsacus, B.C. 405. With scarcely an exception the towns on the mainland and the islands now threw off the Spartan yoke and accepted the autonomy proclaimed by Conon and Pharnabazus as they visited the various places. Though not specially mentioned, there can be little doubt that Cyzicus was among the states which declared against Sparta, for the connection with Athens had been long and intimate. It is not improbable that to this time the present stater may be attributed, and if the figure denotes the victory obtained over the Lacedæmonian fleet, then the inscription would record the freedom gained by the overthrow of the tyranny of Sparta. The theory of M. Charles Lenormant (Rev. Numis., N.S., vol. i. p. 26), and accepted by some writers of authority, notably by his son M. François Lenormant, that it commemorates the Persian defeat by Alexander at the Granicus, B.C. 334, is quite untenable; and, indeed, I do not believe that any of the Cyzicene electrum coins can, with any probability, be assigned to so late a period.

The theory of Millingen, who first published the stater, appears to be equally untenable, but his error is in assigning too early a time for its issue. He thinks that it was struck in commemoration of the victory of the Athenians, under Cimon, over the Persians, when, in B.C. 449, independence was restored to the Greek cities in Asia and the Persian yoke was broken.

A copper coin of Cyzicus, which has on the obverse a head of Persephone, has for its reverse an almost exact copy of the stater type. No wreath is visible, nor is there any inscription on the seat, but ΕΛΕΥΘΕΡΙΑ is placed in front of the figure, inscribed in a single line.

55. Female figure, seated sideways on lion, but to left; she wears a long chiton with sleeves, and, apparently, a turreted crown; her right hand is outstretched over the lion's head, and the left, wrapped in the chiton, rests on her knee. Beneath, tunny left.

Waddington, 247·3 grs. [Pl. III. 4].

*Engr.* Waddington, Voyage en Asie Mineure, Pl. VIII. 2. Rev. Num., xvii. p. 87, Pl. IV. 2.

*Noted.* Brandis, p. 407.

Part of the figure is off the coin, so that it is impossible to say what, if anything, was held in the right hand. The condition also is not sufficiently good to say positively that the figure wears a turreted crown, though there appear to be indications of it. There cannot be any doubt, however, that the Magna Mater, Cybele, is here represented, and accompanied as usual by the great feline beast, her sacred lion. Her worship had spread from Phrygia, and was in early times established in Mysia, where she became largely identified with Rhea. Under the name Dindymene, her chryselephantine statue,[34] which had been carried off from Proconnesus, was preserved at Cyzicus, where she was worshipped under the names Lobrina and Pluciana.

On a frieze lately discovered at Pergamon there is a representation of Cybele seated on a lion.

56. Beardless male head to right, with long flowing hair, wearing necklace and Phrygian bonnet, upon the lappets of which are dotted marks in sets of three. Beneath, tunny right.

W. G. (*a*), 248·4 grs. [Pl. III. 5]. Paris (*b*), 247. Berlin (Fox), 246·8. Munich (*c*), 250.
(*a*), (*b*), (*c*), diff. dies.

*Engr.* Mionnet, Suppl., v., Pl. II. 4. Rev. Num., N.S., vol. i., Pl. II. 2.

*Noted.* Brandis, p. 408.

Hecta. Paris (*a*), 39·5 grs. [Pl. III. 6]. Brit. Mus., 39·2. Paris (De L.) (*b*). Imhoof (*c*), 40·8. Six (*a*), 41.
(*a*), (*b*), (*c*), diff. dies.

*Engr.* Rev. Num., N.S., vol. i., Pl. II. 3.

*Noted.* Brandis, p. 408.

---

[34] The ivory was not elephant's tusk, but of the teeth of the hippopotamus. Pausanias, viii. 46.

The same head, with a tunny beneath, occurs on a silver coin of Cyzicus, which has on the reverse a lion's head with open mouth and the letter ꓧ. All in square incuse. (Rev. Num., N.S., vol. i. Pl. II. 4.)

This very charming head of Atys finds an appropriate place on the coinage of Cyzicus, through his intimate connection with the cult of Cybele.

> 57. Naked male figure, with rounded wings and short tail, and the head of a lion, turned back, kneeling to left; he holds a tunny by the tail in his right hand, his left resting on his side.
>
> W. G. (*a*), 246·7 grs. (Bompois sale, No. 1376). [Pl. III. 7]. St. Pet., 246·8. Imhoof (*b*), 249·5.
> (*a*), (*b*), diff. dies.
>
> *Engr.* Imhoof-Blumer, Choix, Pl. III. 102.
> *Noted.* Imhoof-Blumer, Monn. Grecq., p. 242, No. 71.

A type perhaps impossible to explain with entire satisfaction. The oriental character of the monster is evident, and its occurrence on a coin of Cyzicus may be due to Persian influence. At the same time, in a city of so much commercial enterprise, and which had relations of one kind or another with many and different places, it is not to be wondered that subjects with which the state had no natural or intrinsic connection should be found on its coinage. The type may possibly have been placed on the stater by a magistrate who had trading business with the maritime towns of Phœnicia, where, through earlier intercourse with Assyria, such strange monster forms were familiar. A lion-headed man with eagle's feet occurs frequently among Assyrian sculptures.

Were we to carry back the figure to its first conception, and seek for an explanation of its features, we might recognise the revolution of the sun in its then supposed orbit, and imagine him as just escaping from the bondage of night. The wings and the reverted hand and savage leonine head, with its opened mouth, are all features quite consistent with such an explanation.

Dr. Imhoof-Blumer (Monnaies Grecques, p. 242) regards the figure as Fear ($\Phi \acute{o} \beta o s$). (Milchhöfer, Arch. Zeit, 1881, p. 286). On the chest of Cypselus, the shield of Agamemnon, who is fighting with Coon, had upon it a representation of Fear, with a lion's head.[35]

On the frieze lately discovered at Pergamon, is a lion-headed man.

Among a number of bas-reliefs near the village of Jasili-Kaïa, in ancient Cilicia, which are attributed to the Hittites, are two winged monsters, one a lion-headed man, the other, as M. Perrot thinks, a dog-headed man.[36]

> 58. Winged female figure in rapid motion to left, the head turned back, wearing stephane and a sleeveless chiton, which reaches to the feet; hair represented by dots. She holds a tunny by the tail in the right hand, and in the left the tasselled end of a cord ($\zeta \acute{\omega} \nu \eta$), which is passed round her waist.
>
> Brit. Mus. (*a*), 247·6 grs. (Thomas sale, No. 1774). [Pl. III. 8]. Paris (De L.) (*b*), 247·5.
> (*a*), (*b*), diff. dies.
>
> *Engr.* Annuaire de la Soc. de Num., vol. iv., Pl. VIII. 12. Brit. Mus. Guide, Pl. X. 7. Gardner, Types, Pl. IV. 20.
>
> *Noted.* Brandis, p. 406.

---

[35] Pausanias, lib. v. c. 19.
[36] Explor. Archéol. de la Galatie, &c., par M. Perrot. Pl. XLVIII., reproduced in Histoire de l'art dans l'Antiquité, Perrot et Chipiez, vol. iv. p. 640.

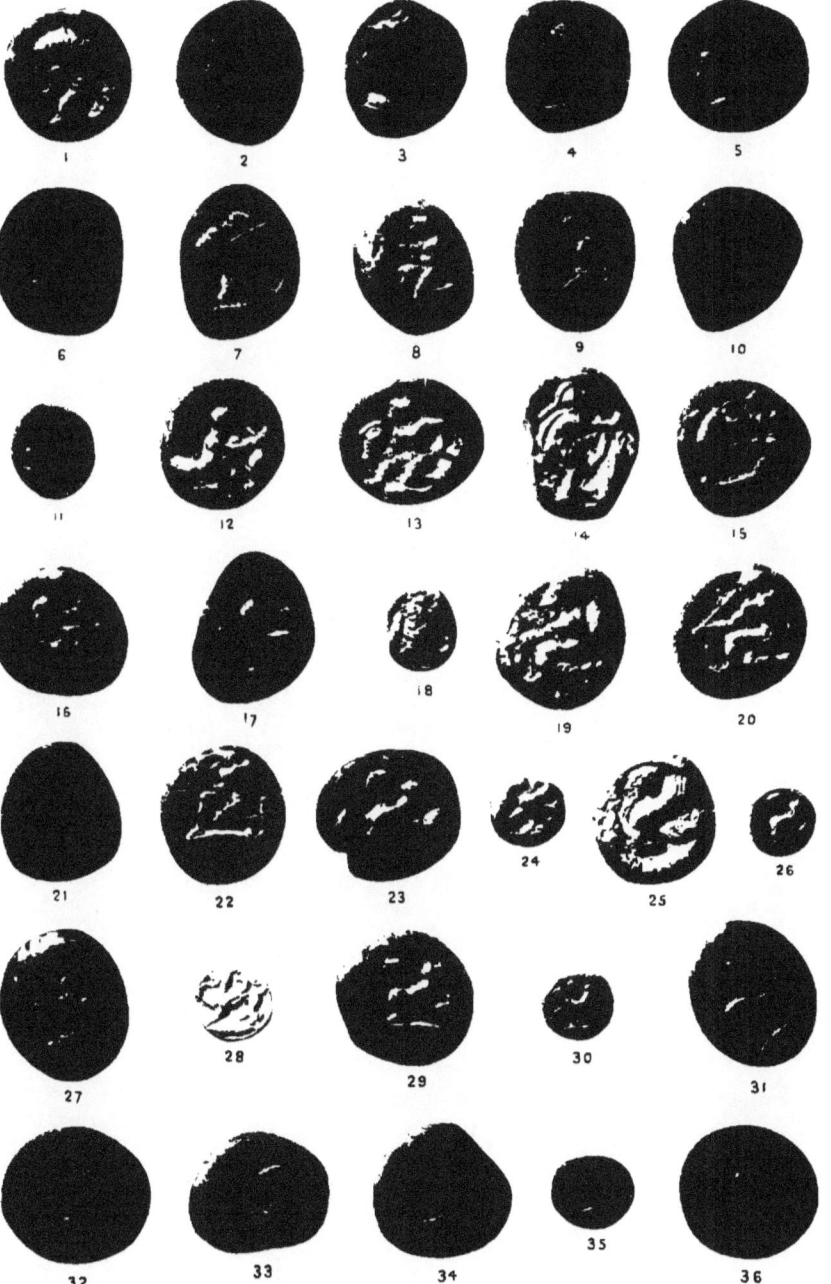

Hecta. Paris (De L.) (*a*), 41·2 grs. [Pl. III. 9].
Brit. Mus. (*b*), 39·6. Paris (*c*), 41·4. Berlin,
40·8. Waddington, 41 (Dupré sale). Iversen,
40·2.

(*a*), (*b*), (*c*), diff. dies.

*Engr.* De Luynes, Choix, Pl. X. 8.

*Noted.* Mionnet, Suppl., ix. p. 280, No. 21.

An archaic coin, and possibly not later than B.C. 500. The figure can scarcely represent Nike, for the action is inconsistent with such an attribution. Like other staters it appears to contain a part only of a larger subject, and with some modifications was, probably, copied from such a group. No coin has up to the present time come to light which might be supposed to supply the complementary part of the subject, but the same is the case in other instances, where there can be no doubt that we have a portion only of a group.

A figure much like that on the coin occurs, on a vase, in association with a scene where Heracles is pursuing Apollo carrying off a hind (Roulez, Choix de vases du Mus. de Leide, p. 31). A similar figure is found on a cylix by Brygos in the British Museum (E. 77), on which is painted Iris seized by Satyrs, Dionysus standing by (Mon. Ined. dell' Inst., ix. Pl. XLVI.). A winged female figure holding a wreath and sceptre, or caduceus, at other times a round disk on which a star is sometimes found, and frequently having the head turned back, occurs on coins of Mallus. M. Waddington (Rev. Num., N.S., vol. v. p. 1, Pl. I.) suggests the figure may be Iris or Nike. Other subjects on the coins of Mallus appear to associate the types with the Syrian Aphrodite-Astarte.

M

59. Naked winged male figure walking to left, holds a tunny by the tail in each hand.

Berlin, 248·4 grs. [Pl. III. 10].

*Engr.* Blätt. für Münz., vol. iv., Pl. XLIV. 1.

A very archaic coin.

The subject, which has not as yet been explained, may possibly be connected with some oriental cult. Koehne, in the account of the stater in Blätter für Münzk., suggests that, perhaps, it is an Eros of very Asiatic type.

60. Winged male figure running to left, holding tunny by the tail.

Twelfth. Brit. Mus., 20 grs. [Pl. III. 11].

The coin is very badly struck, and presents the same difficulty of explanation as the last.

61. Winged male figure, apparently naked, running to left, holds a tunny by the tail in right hand, the left being held up in front of face.

W. G., 249·3 grs. [Pl. III. 12].

Like No. 59 a very archaic coin, and equally difficult to explain.

62. Bearded head, covered with lion's scalp, to right. Beneath, tunny right.

Brit. Mus. (*a*), 246·4 grs. [Pl. III. 13]. Paris (*b*), 247. Berlin (Fox), 246. Moore, 248·5.

(*a*), (*b*), diff. dies.

*Engr.* Fox, Unpubl. Coins, Part II., No. 23.

Head of Heracles, who, as a partaker in the expedition of the Argonauts, becomes connected with Cyzicus, and who is represented in various aspects upon many of the staters. Heracles upon a coin of Trajan, struck at Cyzicus, is called the founder (κτίστης), probably on account of his share in the Argonautic expedition.

63. Two youths, naked, kneeling on tunny left, and turned from each other; the one to left is strangling two serpents, he to right appears to be in the act of imploring aid.

Paris, 247 grs. [Pl. III. 14]. Berlin (Prok.-Ost.), 248·5. Munich, 247. W. G., 247·4. Weber, 248·6.
All from the same die.

*Engr.* Sestini, Stat. Ant. Pl. VI. 12. Prok.-Ost. Ined. (1854), Pl. IV. 2. Rev. Num., N.S. viii., Pl. X. 6.

*Noted.* Mionnet, Suppl., v. p. 369, No. 547.

Hecta. Munich, 40·2 grs. Imhoof, 40·4.
Both same die.

*Engr.* Sestini, Stat. Ant. Pl. VI. 11.

*Noted.* Mionnet, Suppl., v. p. 369, No. 546.

Heracles and his younger brother Iphicles, the former strangling the serpents sent by Hera to destroy them. The subject appears to have been copied from a group in marble, and probably from one forming a metope of a temple.

Among the vases at the Castellani sale (1884) was one (No. 80), which represents Heracles and Iphicles, the latter in the same attitude as on the stater, stretching his hands towards Alcmena, Pallas standing by.

The same subject occurs on a coin of Lampsacus (De Luynes, Ann. dell' Inst. Arch. xiii. p. 150), and the type of Heracles and the serpents, but without his brother, is found on coins of Thebes, and of Samos, Ephesus, Cnidus, Iasus, and Rhodes, states in alliance after the battle of Cnidus, B.C. 394, also on coins of Lampsacus, Croton, Tarentum, and Zacynthus. The type appears to have originated at Thebes, which was the promoter of the resistance to the Spartan hegemony, resulting in its overthrow (B.C. 394—390), and was copied by the first group of states, Samos, &c., as a symbol of confederacy in the cause of independence, and afterwards adopted by Cyzicus, Lampsacus, and other cities.

64. Heracles, youthful, naked, kneeling to right on tunny; he holds a club in his right hand, and in his left a strung bow.

Imhoof (*a*), 245·6 grs. [Pl. III. 15]. Paris (*b*), 248·5. Athens (*b*), 243·7. W. G. (*b*), 247·1 (Whittall sale, 1884, No. 754).
(*a*), (*b*), diff. dies.

65. Bearded figure of Heracles, naked, kneeling right, brandishing a club, held in right hand, over his head, and holding a strung bow and two arrows in his left; hair represented by dots. Behind him, tunny upwards.

Brit. Mus. (*a*), 247·3 grs. [Pl. III. 16]. W. G. (*a*), 249·2. One sold at Sotheby and Wilkinson's, March 22, 1877, No. 101. Another sold at sale of Bank Dupl., Feb. 13, 1878, No. 216.
(*a*), same die.

*Engr.* Num. Chron., N.S., xvii., Pl. VI. 1. Brit. Mus. Guide, Pl. X. 8. Gardner, Types, Pl. IV. 19.

Hecta. Paris (De L.), 40·2 grs.

Though this stater was one of the great find of 1875, it belongs to a much earlier period than the majority of those then discovered. If we may judge from its unworn condition, it does not appear to have been much circulated. We know that the staters were current, but they were no doubt commonly kept as what may be called bank deposits, and were stored to a large amount in the temple treasuries.

Among the gems (Blacas) in the British Museum is a sard, upon one side of which is Heracles, wearing the lion's skin on his back, and holding a club over his head in right hand, and a bow in his outstretched left. On the other side of the stone is Heracles in the garden of the Hesperides.

> 66. Naked bearded figure, seated to left on rock, the head and body partly facing, but inclining to right; he holds a club downwards in his right hand, his left rests on the rock. Beneath, tunny left.
> 
> Berlin (Prok.-Ost.), 245·7 grs. [Pl. III. 17].
> 
> *Engr.* Rev. Num., N.S., ix., Pl. I. 9.

Heracles in the attitude of repose after one of his labours, his club reversed, and his hand resting peacefully behind him. A somewhat similar representation occurs on a coin of Abdera in the Berlin Museum.[37]

> 67. Bearded figure, naked, kneeling left, holding a club over right shoulder in his right hand, and a horn upwards in his left. Behind, tunny upwards.
> 
> W. G. (*a*), 248·4 grs. [Pl. III. 18]. Paris (*b*), 245·7. Weber (*c*), 248·1.
> 
> (*a*), (*b*), (*c*), diff. dies.

Heracles, after his defeat of Achelöus, when he tore off one of his horns, is here represented either holding that horn, or receiving in exchange that of Amaltheia, the well-known horn of plenty.

---

[37] Friedländer, Zeit. für Numis., vol. v. p. 2 (woodcut).

68. Heracles, naked, beardless, kneeling to right on tunny, and holding a club downwards in his right hand, and the lion's skin on his left arm.

Brit. Mus., 247·7 grs. [Pl. III. 19].

*Engr.* Num. Chron., N.S., xvii., Pl. VI. 2.

69. Heracles kneeling right on tunny, and strangling the Nemean lion.

Paris (De L.) (*a*), 247 grs. [Pl. III. 20]. Brit. Mus. (*a*), 247·1. Paris (*a*), 247. W. G. (*a*), 248. Weber, 247·9.

(*a*) same die.

*Engr.* Raoul Rochette, Hercule Assyrien. Pl. III. 6. Num. Chron., N.S., xvi., Pl. VIII. 13.

*Noted.* Brandis, p. 405.

70. Bearded head to left, wearing conical head-dress ($\pi\iota\lambda\iota o\nu$), wreathed with laurel. Beneath, tunny left.

St. Pet. (*a*), 247 grs. [Pl. III. 21]. Paris (De L.) (*b*), 246·8. Ashburnham.

(*a*), (*b*), diff. dies.

*Engr.* Sestini, Stat. Ant., Pl. VI. 2.

*Noted.* Mionnet, Suppl. v., p. 368, No. 542, under Lampsacus. Brandis, p. 408.

This head, which may be, as Professor Gardner suggests (Types, p. 174), of a Cabeirus, is also found on a gold stater of Lampsacus. It has usually been attributed to Odysseus or Hephæstus. The head has not, perhaps, as Mr. Gardner says, " The stately repose which belongs to the divine and consummate artist Hephæstus," but I see no reason why it is not consistent with the crafty, restless, and bold Odysseus, the hero of many wanderings. It looks, indeed, like the head of a storm-tossed, but not weary or disheartened warrior, such as was he who had undergone, but not succumbed to, perils of war on land and of tempests on the sea.

71. Bearded figure, wearing chlamys and conical cap, kneeling to left over a ram, which he is about to slay with a sword, held in his right hand and pointed downwards. Beneath, tunny left.

Berlin (Prok.-Ost.), 245·7 grs. [Pl. III. 22].

*Engr.* Rev. Num., N.S., ix., Pl. I. 10.

*Noted.* Königl. Münz-Kab. (1877), No. 103.

Hecta. Berlin (Prok.-Ost.), 42·4 grs.

This subject, attributed by M. François Lenormant (Rev. Num., N.S., ix. p. 15) to Phrixos sacrificing the ram with the golden fleece, which had carried himself and his sister Helle, is more probably Odysseus, by the advice of Circe, slaying the animal she had provided, before his descent into Hades. The bearded figure is an older person than Phrixos as usually represented, and the head-cover is the cap which Odysseus usually wears. Pausanias, however (Book I., ch. xxiv.), says he saw on the Acropolis at Athens a statue of Phrixos sacrificing a ram to an unknown god, but whom he conjectures to be the same as him to whom the people of Orchomenos gave the name Laphystios, an appellation of Zeus and corresponding to Phyxios.

72. Bearded figure, wearing chlamys which hangs behind, kneeling to left alongside the omphalos, on which his left hand rests; he holds a naked sword upright in his right hand. Beneath, tunny left.

W. G., 246 grs. [Pl. III. 23].

Hecta. Brit. Mus., 38·6 grs.

Orestes at Delphi, after the murder of Aegisthus, before his expiation. The figure, bearded and of mature age, might be supposed to be incompatible with one of

Orestes, who is usually represented as youthful, but on many early vases youths are represented bearded.

Orestes occurs on vases either kneeling or sitting by the omphalos, though not in quite the same position he occupies on the stater. In all these instances he holds a sword.[38] On a marble in the museum at Naples[39] he is represented as a youthful figure, holding a sword and seated near the tripod at Delphi. A female figure, probably his mother, is represented as lying dead, and Apollo holding a bow is placed on a term. Except for the fact that many of the staters present subjects not in any way connected with Cyzicus, so far at least as is known, it might be doubted if Orestes is the person here represented.

73. Head, wearing helmet which terminates at the back in a rounded wing, hair hanging beneath helmet and represented by dots. Behind, tunny downwards.

W. G. (*a*), 248 grs. (Whittall sale, 1884, No. 747). [Pl. III. 24]. Paris (*b*), 248·7. [Pl. III. 25]. Weber (*c*), 248.

(*a*), (*b*), (*c*), diff. dies.

Hecta. Munich, 41 grs.

*Engr.* Sestini, Stat. Ant., Pl. VI. 16.

*Noted.* Mionnet, vi., p. 620, No. 48. Suppl. v., p. 370, No. 550.

This stater, with the head of Perseus, wearing the helmet of Hades lent him by the nymphs, is one of the earliest coins among those of the great find of 1875. The eye is represented as if seen in front, and the hair by dots.

---

[38] Overbeck, Gal. heroischer Bildw., Pl. XXIX. 4, 7, 9, 12.
[39] Mus. Borbon, vol. iv., Pl. 9.

74. Male figure, kneeling left on tunny, with head turned back and covered by a helmet terminating behind in a pointed wing; he wears a chlamys fastened at the neck and folded over the left arm; in his right hand he holds the harpa, and in his left the head of Medusa.

   Paris (De L.), 248·1 grs., [Pl. III. 26]. Waddington, 245·7.

   *Engr.* Mon. Ined. dell' Inst., vol. iii., Pl. XXXV. 23.

   *Noted.* Num. Chron., vi., p. 150, where Mr. Borrell says the helmet is terminated by the head of a vulture. Brandis, p. 406.

   Hecta. Berlin, 41·3 grs.. Imhoof.

Perseus, immediately after slaying Medusa. His attitude betokens expectancy of attack from behind, and he appears to be viewing the Gorgons in pursuit, though there is no indication of fear, the expression being that of confident preparedness. According to Pausanias (v. c. xviii), on the chest of Cypselus there was a representation of the Gorgons pursuing Perseus. He also mentions (i. c. xxii.) a picture in the temple of Nike Apteros at Athens, where Perseus is bringing the head of Medusa to Polydectes at Seriphos.

75. Head of Gorgon. Beneath, tunny left.

   Hecta. Berlin, 41 grs. [Pl. III. 27].

76. Two naked figures running in line to right; the right hand of the figure in front holds a sword prepared to thrust with, and a chlamys hangs over the extended left arm. Beneath, tunny right.

   W. G. (*a*), 247·3 grs. [Pl. III. 28]. Brit. Mus. (*b*), 246. (*a*), (*b*), diff. dies.

   *Engr.* Gardner, Types, Pl. X. 4.

   *Noted.* Num. Vet. R. P. K., p. 109.

Harmodius and Aristogeiton about to kill Hipparchus. The subject, a popular one at Athens, was not unlikely to occur on the coinage of a city so long connected with that state as Cyzicus. It is probably a copy, more or less faithful, of the group by Critios and Nesiotes, which replaced the earlier one by Antenor, carried off by Xerxes, though afterwards restored by Alexander Seleucus or Antiochus. A copy of the original group exists at Naples, though in a much restored form.[40] A similar representation to that on the stater occurs on a tetradrachm of Athens (Beulé, p. 335), and on a Panathenaic vase in the British Museum (B. 637).[41] The usual attitude represents the figure behind holding his sword above his head in the act of striking, and on the stater the same position appears to be intended.

This seems to be the only representation of ordinary mortals appearing on a coin of an early date. The memory of the two brothers was, however, so venerated at Athens that they became invested with more than merely human characteristics, and in that relation were entitled to a position equal to that of semi-deified personages.

77. Head to left, on raised circular disk, wearing earring; the hair, in formal rolls, is represented by dots, and is apparently tied up behind. Beneath, tunny left.

Brit. Mus. (*a*), 248·8 grs. [Pl. III. 29]. Munich (*b*), 247, [Pl. III. 30]. Paris (*c*), 242·7.
(*a*), (*b*), (*c*), diff. dies.

*Engr.* Sestini, Stat. Ant., Pl. V. 1, 2. Dumersan, Cat. Allier, Pl. XII. 8. Rev. Num., N.S., vol. i., Pl. I. 6. Brit. Mus. Guide, Pl. X. 6.

---

[40] Overbeck, Gesch. der Griech. Plastik, i., p. 117, *seq.*, fig. 16.
[41] Mon. Ined. dell' Inst., vol. x., Pl. XLVIII., d.

*Noted.* Num. Vet., R. P. K., p. 134.  Mionnet, vi., p. 617, No. 29.  Brandis, p. 408.

Hecta. Berlin. Munich, 40·7 grs.

*Engr.* Sestini, Stat. Ant., Pl. V. 3, 4.

*Noted.* Mionnet, vol. vi., p. 617, No. 30.

Twelfth. Berlin, 21·3 grs.  St. Pet., 20·7.

*Engr.* Sestini, Stat. Ant., Pl. V. 5.

The head, though wearing an earring, has more of male than of female characteristics, and on a tetradrachm of Amphipolis, Apollo is represented wearing an earring.[42]

The disk is probably that of the Sun, and the head that of Helios, as the Sun-god. It is not radiate, but on the earlier coins of Rhodes the rays are equally wanting. On another stater, No. 23, Helios is represented radiate, and the later Rhodian coins also have a radiate head. Upon a stater of Lampsacus the head of Helios is placed on a radiate disk (Head, Hist. Num., p. 456).

It has been suggested that the head is of a discobolus, placed upon a disc.

78. Male head, with pointed beard, to left; hair hanging long behind and represented by dots. Beneath, tunny left.

Imhoof, 249·8 grs. [Pl. III. 31].

*Engr.* Imhoof-Blumer, Choix, Pl. III. 100.

*Noted.* Imhoof-Blumer, Monn. Grecq., p. 242, No. 69.

Hecta. Paris (two), 41 grs. (*a*), 38·7. Six (*b*), 37·6, plated (Subhi sale, No. 667).

(*a*), (*b*), diff. dies.

*Engr.* Sestini, Stat. Ant., Pl. IX. 25. Rev. Num., N.S., vol. i., Pl. I. 7.

*Noted.* Mionnet, ii., p. 528. No. 80.

An archaic coin, of a head not yet identified.

---

[42] Königl. Münz-Kab., 1877, No. 327.

79. Youthful male head, with short hair, to left. Behind, tunny downwards.

W. G., 245·3 grs. [Pl. III. 32].

This head may possibly, like that on the next stater, be of the hero Cyzicus, but there is nothing distinctive about it to enable us to attach it to any god or hero.

80. Youthful male head to left. Beneath, tunny left.

Paris (two), 243·6 grs. (*a*) [Pl. IV. 1], 246·7. Brit. Mus. (*b*), 243·6. W. G. (*a*), 245·8. (Subhi sale, No. 211). Lambros.
(*a*), (*b*), diff. dies.

*Engr.* Num. Chron., N.S. xvi., Pl. VIII. 11.

*Noted.* Brandis, p. 408.

The absence of a wreath is inconsistent with the head being attributed to Apollo or Dionysus. As has been suggested by Mr. Head (Num. Chron., N.S., xvi. p. 281), it may be of the hero Cyzicus, whose head, wearing a diadem, and with his name, is frequently found on copper coins of the state.

81. Bald, bearded and laureate head to right. Beneath, tunny right.

W. G. (*a*), 245·9 grs. (Thomas sale, No. 1912. Northwick, No. 955. Paravey, No. 187). [Pl. IV. 2]. Paris (De L.) (*b*), 247·5. [Pl. IV. 3]. Paris, 242·7. Berlin, 246·8.
(*a*), (*b*), diff. dies.

*Engr.* Sestini, Stat. Ant., Pl. V. 20. Mionnet, Pl. XLIII. 1. Num. Chron., N.S., xx., Pl. I. 10. Gardner, Types, p. 175, Pl. X. 42.

*Noted.* Brandis, p. 408. Königl. Münz-Kab. (1877), No. 105.

A most remarkable coin, and one which presents grave difficulties in its explanation. On account of the time at which it must have been struck, it is perhaps impossible, notwithstanding the exceptional scope of the Cyzicene representations, to consider it as intended to portray any individual personage of however exalted a position. At the same time it must be remembered that there is, upon a coin attributed to Colophon, as well as on others, a head which can scarcely be regarded as other than a portrait, though Professor Gardner (Types of Greek Coins, p. 144) believes it to be the idealised head of a Persian king. But whoever the artist of the Cyzicene stater meant to represent, there can be little doubt he modelled the portrait from the life.

82. Youthful, beardless, male head to right, wearing a wreath of laurel? Beneath, tunny right.
    Paris, 247 grs. [Pl. IV. 4].
    *Noted.* Brandis, p. 408.

This head, which appears to wear a wreath of laurel, may possibly be of Apollo, though it is certainly not one characteristic of the god.

83. Youthful, beardless, male head to left, with short hair and wearing tænia tied over the forehead. Beneath, tunny left.
    Paris (De L.) (*a*), 246·5 grs. [Pl. IV. 5]. Paris (*b*), 248·6. Berlin (Fox), 247. (Thomas sale, No. 1911).
    (*a*), (*b*), diff. dies.
    *Engr.* Fox, Unpubl. Coins, ii. No. 24.
    *Noted.* Königl. Münz-Kab. (1877), No. 104.

One of the latest issues of the staters. It is very similar to the head of Dionysus on a coin of Timotheus, dynast of Heraclea, in Bithynia.

84. Female head to left. Beneath, tunny left.
    Lewis, 245·5 grs. [Pl. IV. 6]. Weber, 246·6.

85. Female head to right, wearing earring, and with head in saccos drawn together at the top, and ornamented with a mæander pattern above and a zigzag. Beneath, tunny right.
    W. G., 246·9 grs. (Whittall sale, 1884, No. 759). [Pl. IV. 7]. Six, 248·3.

The head on this stater is a direct copy from that on a well-known tetradrachm of Syracuse, similar to No. 112, Cat. of Sicilian Coins, in the British Museum. It is one of the many proofs, and a most convincing one, that Cyzicus reproduced on its coinage the types of other and sometimes remote states.

86. Naked figure, bearded, kneeling to left, holds a tunny by the tail in his right hand, his left resting on his right thigh.
    Paris, 251·4 grs. [Pl. IV. 8]. Brit. Mus., 248·7.
    Diff. dies.
    *Engr.* Num. Chron., N.S., xvii., Pl. VI. 4.
    *Noted.* Num. Chron., vi., p. 151. Brandis, p. 405.
    Hecta. Brit. Mus. (*a*), 36·9 grs. Paris, 40·2. Munich (*b*), 41. Vienna (*c*), 42·3. Berlin (three), (Prok.-Ost.), 40·1. (Fox), 41. (Sperling), 39·7. Six (*a*), 41·5. Bunbury, 40. Weber (*d*), 41·6. W. G. (*b*), 40·9. (Whittall sale, 1884, No. 351). R. and F., 39·4.
    (*a*), (*b*), (*c*), (*d*), diff. dies.
    *Engr.* Sestini, Stat. Ant., Pl. V. 10.
    *Noted.* Mionnet, vi., p. 616, No. 22.
    Twelfth. Paris, 18·6 grs. Berlin (three), 20·6, 20·5, 19·5. Munich, 20·5.
    *Engr.* Sestini, Stat. Ant., Pl. V. 11.
    *Noted.* Mionnet, vi., p. 616, No. 23.

87. Naked male figure, half-kneeling to left, holding a tunny by the tail in each hand.

W. G., 247 grs. [Pl. IV. 9]. Lambros in 1885.

*Engr.* Num. Chron., N.S., xx., Pl. I. 9.

A coin of an earlier date than the greater number of those of the find of 1875, of which I believe, though I have no certain proof, it formed a part. The exaggerated way in which the muscles are expressed is very characteristic of early work, and is well shown on the stater. The subject is one, like the last and many others, which seems beyond explanation.

88. Male figure, naked, beardless, kneeling right, wearing tænia; he holds in his right hand, which hangs down by his side, a large knife downwards, and on his extended left hand a tunny.

W. G., 248·1 grs. [Pl. IV. 10]. Brit. Mus., 246·4. Hunter, 248·4.
All diff. dies.

*Engr.* Hunter, Pl. LXVI. 1. Sestini, Stat. Ant., Pl. V. 8. Num. Chron., N.S., xvii., Pl. VI. 3.

*Noted.* Mionnet, vi., p. 616, No. 21.

Hecta. The Hague (*a*). [Pl. IV. 11]. Brit. Mus. (two), 41 grs., (*b*), 40·3. Paris (De L.), 41. Berlin (Prok.-Ost.), 40·7. Imhoof (*c*), 41·5. Six (*d*), 41·4. Waddington (Dupré sale), 41·3. Carfrae (*e*), 40·5. W. G. (*a*), 40·3.
(*a*), (*b*), (*c*), (*d*), (*e*), diff. dies.

*Engr.* Sestini, Stat. Ant., Pl. V. 9. De Luynes, Choix, Pl. X. 9 (incorrectly).

*Noted.* Mionnet, Suppl., v., p. 303, No. 120.

Upon some of the hectæ the tænia is very visible, and the prominence of the spike over the forehead gives the head somewhat of the appearance of having a horn.

89. Child, naked, seated facing, but turned to right, resting on his left arm, and holding a tunny by the tail in his right hand.

Brit. Mus., 245·9 grs. [Pl. IV. 12]. Paris, 247.
Diff. dies.

*Engr.* Mionnet, Suppl., v., Pl. III. 2. Num. Chron., N.S. xvii., Pl. VI. 5.

*Noted.* Mionnet, vi., p. 615, No. 19. Suppl., v., p. 301, No. 110. Brandis, p. 405.

Possibly a figure of the youthful Heracles.

90. Naked male figure, kneeling to left on tunny; he is stooping forward, and holds on his right arm a crested helmet, and in his left hand a short sword.

W. G. (*a*), 244·5 grs. (Whittall sale, 1884, No. 745). [Pl. IV. 13]. Brit. Mus. (*b*), 246. Berlin. Waddington, 246·9. R. and F. One sold at Whittall sale (1884), No. 746.
(*a*), (*b*), diff. dies.

*Engr.* Num. Chron., N.S., xvi., Pl. VIII. 16.

Hecta. Brit. Mus., 41·7 grs. (Huber sale). Berlin, 41·2.

Mr. Head, in his paper on the coins of the find of 1875 (Num. Chron., N.S., xvi., p. 282), suggests that this figure may be one of the Argonauts, and the attribution is not improbable, the mythical history of Cyzicus being so closely connected with their expedition.

91. Male figure, naked, in a stooping position to right, wearing a crested helmet from which a plume projects behind, on his left arm he holds a round shield, his right being outstretched over a tunny downwards.

Imhoof (*a*), 246 grs. [Pl. IV. 14]. Brit. Mus. (*b*), 246·3. Paris (De L.), (*c*), 245·7. Bunbury (Dupré sale, No. 252). Jones. W. G. (*d*), 249·8. Lambros in 1885.
(*a*), (*b*), (*c*), (*d*), diff. dies.

*Noted.* Num. Vet., R. P. K., p. 45. Brandis, p. 406.
Hecta. Paris (De L.), 42·8 grs. Copenhagen.
*Engr.* De Luynes, Choix, Pl. X. 7.
*Noted.* Brandis, p. 406.

This figure perhaps represents a statue of a hoplite who has either been victorious in a race and extends his hand to receive the prize, or else one who is preparing for the race. Cf. a kylix at Leyden, on which a victorious hoplite stands, in the same attitude, at the goal; he carries a shield on which is a running hoplite. Cf. also Bull. Napol. N.S. VI. Taf. 7; Mitth. d. arch. Inst. 1880, Pl. XIII.; and Pausanias I. 23, 9 (statue of Epicharinus).

> 92. Male figure, naked, kneeling left on tunny; he is advancing a round shield on his left arm, and is apparently about to thrust with sword or spear, held in his right hand.

Paris, 247 grs. [Pl. IV. 15].

*Engr.* Raoul-Rochette, Mem. d'Arch. comp. Sur l'Hercule Assyrien. Pl. II. 17.

The coin is double struck and in poor condition.

The warrior, whoever he may be, appears to be awaiting the attack of an enemy, and covers himself from the approaching lance or sword-thrust with his shield. This may be another instance where a part has been selected from a larger subject, such as one of Centaurs and Lapithæ, or of Greeks and Amazons. M. Waddington[43] gives an engraving of a coin attributed to the Satrap Orontes, where a warrior, with a conical head-dress and armed with a spear, shelters himself behind his shield. He thinks it may represent the Athenian general Chabrias, who introduced a system of tactics against an attacking

---

[43] Rev. Num., N.S., viii., Pl. XI. 5. The coin is also figured, De Luynes, Satrapies, Pl. VIII. 1.

enemy, in which the shield was placed on the ground, and whose statue represented him in the same attitude. Bronze coins of the Tauric Chersonesus have a similar subject and treated in a similar way. The stater, however, cannot be attributed to so late a time as that of Chabrias, who was killed B.C. 357, and although he introduced a certain method of resisting an attack by placing the shield of the hoplite on the ground instead of its being held higher, the attitude is one which must have been commonly used to resist an individual attack, if it was not one where a larger body of men was employed. The position is a quite common one upon Assyrian sculptures, where native soldiers, and what may be Carian mercenaries, are represented sheltering behind their shields fixed on the ground.

98. Male figure, naked, wearing crested Corinthian helmet, kneeling to right; he holds an arrow with both hands, along which he appears to be looking to see if it is straight, before adjusting it to the bow, which hangs upon his left wrist. Behind, tunny downwards.

Brit. Mus. (two), (*a*), Num. Chron., N.S., xvi., Pl. VIII. 17, 247 grs. [Pl. IV. 16], (*b*), l. c., Pl. VIII. 18., 248·2. W. G. (*c*), 247. [Pl. IV. 17]. Paris (*b*), 246·4. Berlin (Prok.-Ost.), 246·8. Waddington, 248·8.

(*a*), (*b*), (*c*), diff. dies.

*Engr.* Sestini, Stat. Ant., Pl. V. 7. Mionnet, Pl. XLIII. 8. Num. Chron., N.S., xvi., Pl. VIII., 17, 18. Gardner, Types, Pl. X. 5.

*Noted.* Mionnet, ii., p. 527, No. 77.

Hecta. Vienna, 40·6 grs. [Pl. IV. 18]. Iversen, 41·5, (found at Kertch).

*Engr.* Eckhel., Mus. Cæs. Vind. Sylloge., i., p. 76, Tab. VII. 5. Sestini, Stat. Ant., Pl. V. 12.

*Noted.* Mionnet, Suppl. v., p. 303, No. 119.

94. Similar to the last, but the warrior kneels to left, and the tunny is upwards.

W. G. (*a*), 245·9 grs. (Bompois sale, No. 1,378). [Pl. IV. 19]. Löbbecke (*b*), 248·7. [Pl. IV. 20]. St. Pet. (two), 246·32, (*c*), 247.
(*a*), (*b*), (*c*), diff. dies.

*Noted.* Zeit. für Numis., x. (1882), p. 76, No. 25.

Jason and the Argonauts are prominent actors in the mythical history of Cyzicus, and the warrior represented on this and the preceding coin may be Jason or one of his band.

95. Male figure, wearing cloak, trousers, and boots, seated right on tunny; over his left wrist hangs a strung bow, and in his right hand he holds an arrow, which he appears to be examining.
St. Pet. 247 grs. [Pl. IV. 21].

This stater is of very good work, and of more than common interest. The dress of the warrior is characteristic of a Scythian, and corresponds with frequent representations of those people on vases and other works. It may be compared with the two staters last described (Nos. 93, 94), where a Greek warrior is engaged upon the same operation with his arrow, and holds the bow in the same position.

The subject appears to be another link between Cyzicus and Panticapæum and the Hyperborean regions, but it may also have its place on the coinage of Cyzicus in connection with the Argonautic expedition.

96. Male figure, naked, kneeling left on tunny, holds a lance(?) in right hand and in his left a sword, point upwards, held by the blade, the hilt projecting beyond the hand.
Berlin, 247·3 grs. [Pl. IV. 22].

97. Harpy, standing left and holding a tunny by the tail in right hand; two objects like vine tendrils project from the back of the head.

W. G., 245·8 grs. (Whittall sale, 1884, No. 752). [Pl. IV. 23]. Waddington, 247·5.

Hecta. Imhoof, 41 grs. [Pl. IV. 24].

*Engr.* Millingen, Sylloge, Pl. III. 39. De Luynes, Choix, Pl. X. 8.

The peculiar object which projects from the back of the head is also found attached to the head of the Sphinx. The very early representations of that creature on ivory combs and plaques discovered at Spata have the head covered with the mitre, to which, at the back, are attached short plumes (?), with curled ends, and beyond them a long streamer, which seems to float in the wind.[44] It may be remarked that it is only where the whole creature is represented on the staters and hectæ that these appendages are found; where only the forepart of Harpy or Sphinx, Nos. 98, 102, forms the type, they are absent.

98. Forepart of Harpy to left, holding a tunny by the tail in right hand.

Hirsch., 249·7 grs. [Pl. IV. 25].

Hecta. Paris, 30·2. [Pl. IV. 26].

Twelfth. Paris, 20·2 grs.

*Engr.* Dumersan, Cat. Allier, Pl. XII. 6. Mionnet, Suppl., ix., Pl. X. 4.

*Noted.* Mionnet, Suppl., v., p. 303, No. 122, but he calls it a Sphinx and places it to right. His reference is to Dumersan.

---

[44] Bull. de Corresp. Hellén., vol. ii., Pl. XVII. 1, 2. Pl. XVIII. 1.

99. Sphinx standing to left on tunny, the right fore-paw raised ; a plume or other object with two curled ends projects from the back of head.

Brit. Mus. (*a*), 243·4 grs. [Pl. IV. 27]. Waddington (Dupré sale), 245·8. W. G. (*a*), 246·3. Weber (*a*).
(*a*) same die.

*Engr.* Num. Chron., N.S., xvii., Pl. VI. 7.

*Noted.* Brandis, p. 400, under Chios, who appears to confuse the standing and seated Sphinx.

Hecta. St. Pet. (*a*), 41·5 grs. [Pl. IV. 28]. Berlin (Prok.-Ost.), 41·5. Imhoof (*b*).
(*a*), (*b*), diff. dies.

*Engr.* Dumersan, Cat. Allier, Pl. XVI. 1. Sestini, Stat. Ant., Pl. IX. 8. Mionnet, Pl. XLIII. 11. Prokesch-Osten, Ined., 1854, Pl. IV. 6.

*Noted.* Mionnet, iii., p. 265, No. 1. Brandis, p. 400.

The Sphinx is the long-continued coin-type of Chios, and its occurrence on the staters and hectæ of Cyzicus may be nothing more than the reproduction on its own coinage of the type of another state. In connection, however, with Dionysus the Sphinx would not be one unlooked for among the many and varied types of the Cyzicene coinage.

99\*. Sphinx, with pointed wing, standing left, right fore-paw raised. Beneath, tunny left.

W. G., 246·4 grs.

This stater formed one of the coins found at the Piræus in 1882, but it became known to the author too late to be figured in the plates.

100. Sphinx seated left on tunny, the right fore-paw raised ; hair represented by dots ; it has the usual projection behind the head.

Paris (De L.), 247 grs. [Pl. IV. 29].

*Engr.* Rev. Num., N.S., vol. i., Pl. I. 8.

Hecta. Paris (two), 41 grs., 41. Munich (*a*), 41. Six (*a*), 40·7. (Ivanoff sale, No. 160). W. G. (*a*), 41·8.
(*a*) same die.

Twelfth. Gotha, 20·2 grs.

101. Sphinx seated, head facing, with two bodies; the usual projection behind the head.

Paris, 43·4 grs. [Pl. IV. 30].

*Engr.* Brönsted, Voy. en Grèce, vol. ii., p. 158, vign. xli. Mionnet, Suppl., ix., Pl. X. 5.

*Noted.* Brandis, p. 400, under Chios.

Cousinéry (Voy. dans la Macédoine, i., p. 99) describes a terra-cotta with a similar representation, found at Pella. It is possible that this treatment of the Sphinx is merely a way of representing it as seen facing, arising from the difficulty of depicting a figure in that position. A somewhat similar mode is found on the archaic figures of Nike flying, on Sicilian coins, where the wings are spread on each side of the body instead of appearing behind it.

102. Forepart of Sphinx to left, the right fore-paw raised. Beneath, tunny left.

Brit. Mus. (*a*), 248·6 grs. (Subhi sale, No. 762). [Pl. IV. 31]. Paris (*b*), 248·5. W. G. (*b*), 246·6.
(*a*), (*b*), diff. dies.

*Engr.* Rev. Num., N.S., vol. i., Pl. I. 5.

*Noted.* Brandis, p. 400, under Chios.

Hecta. W. G., 40·1 grs. (Whittall sale, 1884, No. 762).

103. Lion standing left on tunny, with closed mouth, and tail turned outwards.

W. G. (*a*), 247·1 grs. (Von Rauch coll.). [Pl. IV. 32]. St. Pet. (*a*), 245·8. Leake (*b*), 246·5.
(*a*), (*b*), diff. dies.

*Engr.* Head, Hist. Num. Fig. 278.

*Noted.* Leake, Num. Hellen. Suppl., p. 44.

The lion or lioness appears under various aspects upon the staters. The animal is represented whole or dimidiated, to use heraldic language, walking, sitting, devouring his prey and breaking a weapon with his teeth, and winged. It occurs usually alone, but also as forming part of a subject, and sometimes there is merely the head.

The lion is connected in so many ways with Hellenic mythology, and especially where it became influenced by Asiatic cults, that it is, perhaps, impossible to associate any individual coin-subject with a particular myth, except in connection with Heracles. The lion as a sun-symbol, and so associated with the god of day and light, would be a quite natural type on the coinage of Cyzicus, and to this we may, perhaps, attribute its frequent occurrence. In connection with Cybele the lion may equally be expected on the coins of a state which by its position was brought into intimate relation with the worship of the goddess. It may also have reference to the cult of Astarte-Aphrodite, who, however, herself is, more or less, to be identified with Cybele.

104. Lion standing left on tunny, with open mouth and tail turned inwards.

Paris, 246·8 grs. [Pl. IV. 83]. Copenhagen, 245·7, (Thomas sale, No. 1915; Huxtable sale, No. 149).
Diff. dies.

*Engr.* Sestini, Stat. Ant., Pl. IV. 16. Mionnet, Pl. XLIII. 7.

*Noted.* Mionnet, ii. p. 527, No. 76.

105. Lion, with open mouth, seated left on tunny, the right fore-paw raised.

Brit. Mus., 246·8 grs. [Pl. IV. 84].

Hecta. Brit. Mus. (*a*), 41 grs. [Pl. IV. 35]. Paris (*a*), 41. Paris (De L.) (two), 41·7 (*b*), 41·4. Berlin. Munich (*b*), 41·4. St. Pet., 41·7. Leake, 41·9. W. G. (*a*), 41·2. Prince of Windisch-Grätz, 41·8.
(*a*), (*b*), diff. dies.

*Engr.* Sestini, Stat. Ant., Pl. IV. 19, 20.

*Noted.* Mionnet, Suppl., v. p. 302, Nos. 115, 116. Leake, Num. Hell. Suppl., p. 44.

Twelfth. Brit. Mus., 21·2 grs.

*Engr.* Sestini, Stat. Ant., Pl. IV. 21.

*Noted.* Mionnet, Suppl., v. p. 302, No. 117.

106. Lioness standing left on tunny, the right fore-paw raised, the tail turned up over back.

Weber (*a*), 248·9 grs. [Pl. IV. 36]. Berlin (*b*), 248·8. Hoffmann (fruste), 230.
(*a*), (*b*), diff. dies.

*Noted.* Königl. Münz-Kab. (1877), No. 101.

Hecta. Munich, 30·8 grs. St. Pet., 40·5. Hirsch, 39·4. W. G., 40·2 (Whittall sale, 1884, No. 760).
All diff. dies.

*Engr.* Sestini, Stat. Ant., Pl. VIII. 16.

107. Lion to left, apparently devouring his prey. Beneath, tunny left.

Brit. Mus. (*a*), 247 grs. [Pl. V. 1]. Paris (De L.), 246·5. W. G. (*a*), 246·6.
(*a*), same die.

*Engr.* Sestini, Stat. Ant., Pl. IV. 18. Num. Chron., N.S., xvii., Pl. VI. 6.

*Noted.* Mionnet, Suppl., v. p. 302, No. 113. Brandis, p. 408.

Hecta. Paris (De L.) (*a*), 41·3 grs. Berlin (two), Fox, 41, Prok.-Ost., 40·8. Vienna (*b*), 40·4. Leake (*b*), 40·7.
(*a*), (*b*), diff. dies.

*Noted.* Brandis, p. 408.

Twelfth. Paris (*a*), 20·1 grs. Vienna, 22·7. St. Pet. (*a*), 24.
(*a*), same die.

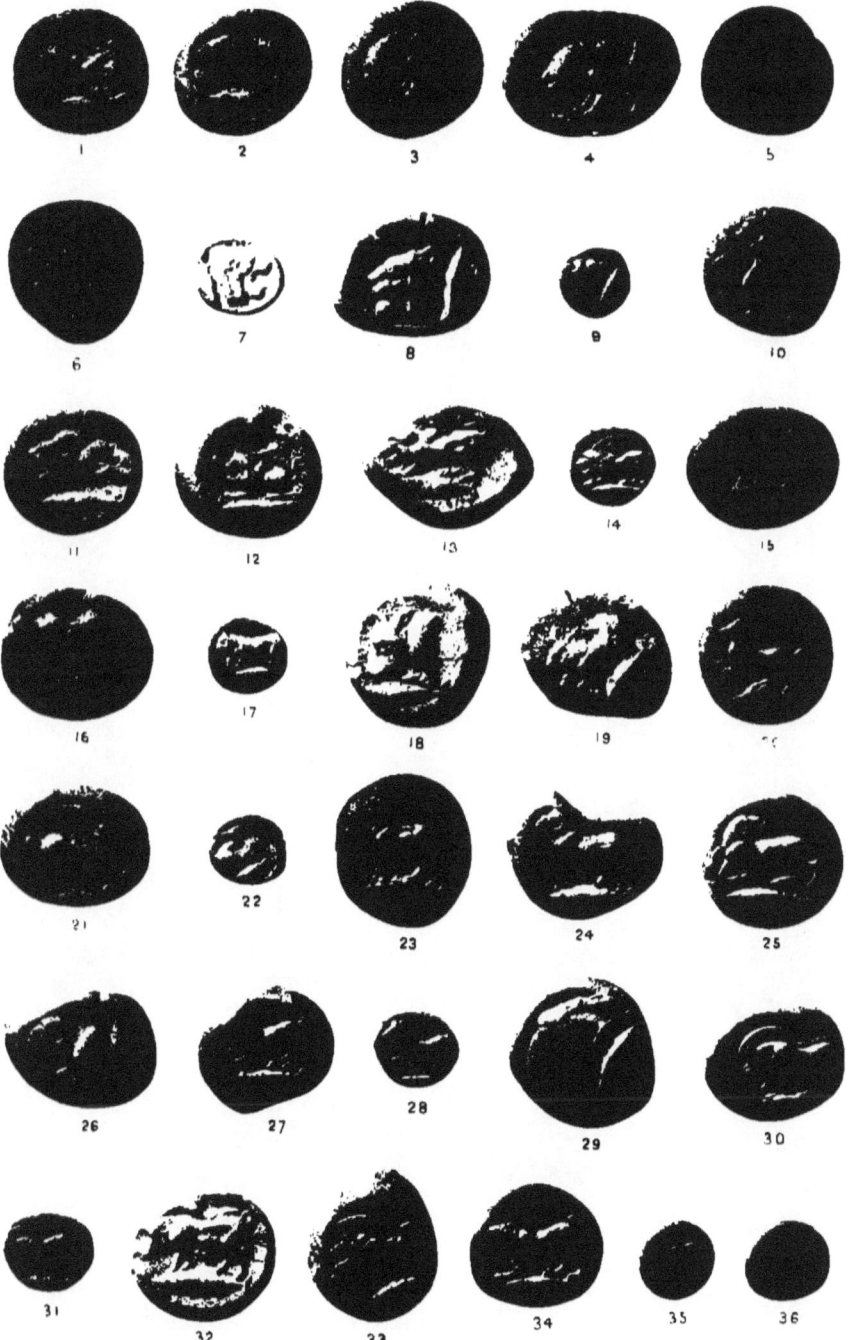

108. Lion standing to right, with tail between his legs, holds the hilt of a weapon with his right fore-paw, and is biting the blade, which projects beyond his mouth. Beneath, tunny right.

W. G., 245·4 grs. [Pl. V. 2]. St. Pet., 245·7.
Diff. dies.

*Engr.* Rev. de la Num. Belg., vol. ii., Pl. V. 8.

Hecta. Imhoof, 39·6 grs.

The weapon held by the lion is curved, and has more the appearance of the harpa of Perseus than of a sword. Mr. Burgon, the author of the Catalogue of the Thomas Collection, where a similar coin formed lot 1914, was of the opinion that it was the harpa, but, acknowledging the unlikeliness of such a representation, withheld his judgment until another coin turning up, might give a better impression of the die. It is unfortunate that upon neither of the two coins at present known to me, is the end of the weapon quite distinct, still there is sufficient shown to make it almost certain that it is the harpa, a fact which would connect it with the myth of Perseus.

109. Forepart of lioness to left, apparently devouring her prey. Behind, tunny upwards.

Brit. Mus. (*a*), 247·8 grs. (Subhi sale, No. 1150). [Pl. V. 3]. Imhoof (*b*), 248·3. [Pl. V. 4]. W. G. (*b*), 247·7. Lambros, in 1885 (two).
(*a*), (*b*), diff. dies.

*Engr.* Imhoof-Blumer, Choix, Pl. III. 101.

Hecta. Berlin, 40·2 grs. Munich, 39·7. Imhoof, 39·5.
All diff. dies.

*Engr.* Sestini, Stat. Ant., Pl. IV. 22.

*Noted.* Mionnet, Suppl., v. p. 304, No. 123.

Twelfth. Paris (De L.). Vienna (*a*), 22·5 grs. St. Pet. (*b*), 20·1. Six (*c*).
(*a*), (*b*), (*c*), diff. dies.

*Engr.* De Luynes, Choix, Pl. X. 12.

On the hecta and twelfth the object held in the mouth is much like a bone. The type is found on silver coins, probably of Phocæa, many of which have been found in Southern Italy and near Marseilles.

110. Forepart of lion to left, with open mouth, the head turned back. Behind, tunny downwards.

W. G., 248·3 grs. [Pl. V. 5].

111. Forepart of lioness to left, the head turned back. Behind, tunny.[45]

Berlin, 41 grs. Waddington, 40·8.

112. Head and neck of lioness to left, with paw. Behind, tunny.

Waddington, 20·1 grs.

113. Lion's scalp, facing. Beneath, tunny left.

W. G., 248·4 grs. (Whittall sale, No. 1044). [Pl. V. 6]. Brit. Mus. 250·5.
       Both the same die.

*Engr.* Num. Chron., N.S., xvi., Pl. VIII. 26. Brit. Mus. Guide, Pl. X. 13.

Hecta. Brit. Mus. (*a*), 41·2 grs. Paris (two), 42·4, (*a*), 41·5. Berlin (three), (Fox, two), (Prok.-Ost.). Six (*a*).
       (*a*), same die.

*Engr.* Sestini, Stat. Ant., Pl. IV. 6. Mionnet, Suppl., ix., Pl. X. 9.
*Noted.* Mionnet, vi. p. 614, No. 9. Brandis, p. 401, under Samos.

A copy of the ordinary type of Samos.

---

[45] I was not acquainted with this hecta, nor with the twelfth, No. 112, in time to enable me to include them in the plates.

114. Head of lion, with open mouth to right. Behind, tunny downwards.

Munich, 41·3 grs. [Pl. V. 7].

*Noted.* Mionnet, vol. vi. p. 614, No. 7.

115. Head of lioness, mouth closed, to left. Behind, tunny upwards.

Imhoof (*a*), 250 grs. [Pl. V. 8]. Brit. Mus. (*b*), 248. Paris, 247. W. G. (*b*), 248·4.
(*a*), (*b*), diff. dies.

*Engr.* Num. Chron., N.S., xvii., Pl. VI. 10.

*Noted*, Brandis, p. 404.

Hecta. Paris, 40·1 grs. Paris (De L.) (two), 40, 39. Berlin (Prok.-Ost.). Six, 41·3. Moore, 39·5. Weber, 40·6 (Whittall sale, 1884, No. 1002).

*Noted.* Brandis, p. 404.

116. Head of lioness, facing. In field to left tunny downwards.

Brit. Mus., 41 grs. [Pl. V. 9].

117. Forepart of winged lioness to left. Behind, tunny upwards.

Paris, 247·6 grs. [Pl. V. 10].

*Engr.* Dumersan, Cat. Allier, Pl. XII. 3.

*Noted.* Mionnet, Suppl., v. p. 300, No. 104. Brandis, p. 404.

It will be seen from the types on other coins that winged creatures occur frequently on the coinage of Cyzicus. Here it is a winged lioness, and there are bulls, boars, and dogs, without taking Pegasus into account. These representations are no doubt Oriental in their origin, and probably denote motion, in connection with Solar worship.

118. Head of lion to left, head of ram to right, joined at the neck. Beneath, tunny left.

Löbbecke, 247·4 grs. [Pl. V. 11]. W. G., 247·6. Diff. dies.

*Noted.* Zeit. für Numis. (1882), vol. x. p. 76, No. 24.

Twelfth. Paris (De L.), 20·5 grs.

*Engr.* Ann. dell' Inst. Archeol., vol. xiii., p. 150, Mon. Pl. XXXV. 21.

A type similar in some respects to the early Lydian stater, with the forepart of lion and bull conjoined in the same manner, which are supposed to symbolise the sun and moon.

119. Chimæra seated to left, with open mouth, and tail ending in a serpent's head. Beneath, tunny left.

Brit. Mus., 254·1 grs. [Pl. V. 12].

The chimæra on this stater does not seem to have the head of a lion, as the monster is ordinarily represented, but on the stater next to be described that feature is quite apparent.

The chimæra appears upon an early electrum coin, attributed by Mr. Head (Num. Chron., N.S., vol. xv. p. 285) to Zeleia, a town which at one time was included within the territory of Cyzicus. Though the ordinary type of Sicyon, it is scarcely likely that this is one of the cases where Cyzicus reproduced a subject from the coinage of another state. As connected with the Bellerophon myth, we might expect to find it upon the Cyzicene coinage.

120. Chimæra standing to left, with open mouth. Beneath, tunny left.

Imhoof, 247·2 grs. [Pl. V. 13].

*Engr.* Imhoof-Blumer, Choix, Pl. III. 98.

*Noted.* Imhoof-Blumer, Monn. Grecq., p. 241, No. 66.

Hecta. Paris, 40 grs. [Pl. V. 14].

*Engr.* Sestini, Stat. Ant., Pl. V. 19. Mionnet, Pl. XLIII. 8. Dumersan, Cat. Allier, Pl. VI. 14. Lajard, Culte de Vénus, Pl. III., B. 20.

*Noted.* Mionnet, Suppl., iv. p. 160, No. 1047. Num. Chron., vi. p. 136. Brandis, p. 404.

121. Bull walking left. Beneath, tunny left.

Brit. Mus. (*a*), 248·5 grs. [Pl. V. 15]. Paris, 247. St. Pet. (*a*), 246·8. Imhoof (*a*), 247. Weber, 247·8 (Whittall sale, 1884, No. 751). W. G. (*b*), 247·3. Jones. Hoffmann, 246·9.

(*a*), (*b*), diff. dies.

*Engr.* Num. Chron., N.S., xvi., Pl. VIII. 28. Brit. Mus. Guide, Pl. X. 11.

*Noted.* Num. Vet. R. P. K., p. 95. Num. Chron., vi. p. 150. Leake, Num. Hell. Asiat. Greece, p. 50. Brandis, p. 388, under Chalcedon.

Hecta. Berlin (Fox), 41 grs.

Twelfth. Berlin, 21·3 grs.

Brandis classes this stater to Chalcedon, but the presence of the tunny compels it to be given to Cyzicus. The bull occurs on the coinage of other cities as well as of Byzantium and Chalcedon, and Cyzicus may have taken this type from any one of them. As has already been noticed in the introduction, Dionysus had a statue at Cyzicus in the form of a bull.

122. Bull butting to right. Beneath, tunny right.

Brit. Mus. (*a*), 247·1 grs. [Pl. V. 16]. W. G. (*a*), 247 (Bompois sale, No. 1362). Weber (*b*), 247·8. Lambros (*b*), 247.

(*a*), (*b*), diff. dies.

*Engr.* Num. Chron., N.S., xvi., Pl. VIII. 27.

A copy of the ordinary type of Thurium. We have an instance of Cyzicus taking a coin-type from a city quite as far distant in No. 85, where a coin of Syracuse served for the model.

123. Ox kneeling or lying down to left. Beneath, tunny left.
Brit. Mus., 40 grs. [Pl. V. 17].
*Engr.* Sestini, Stat. Ant., Pl. IV. 24.
*Noted.* Mionnet, Suppl., v. p. 304, No. 124.

124. Head of bull to left. Beneath, tunny left.
Brit. Mus., 247·5 grs. [Pl. V. 18].
*Engr.* Num. Chron., N.S., xvi., Pl. VIII. 29.

125. Forepart of winged bull galloping to left. Beneath, tunny left.
W. G., 246·3 grs. [Pl. V. 19]. Brit. Mus., 247·5. Lambros in 1885.
All from the same die.
Twelfth. Paris (De L.), 20·1 grs.
*Engr.* Ann. dell' Inst. Archeol., vol. xiii., Pl. XXXV. 22.

126. Horse galloping to left, reins hanging loose. Beneath, tunny left.
St. Pet., 246·5 grs. [Pl. V. 20]. Berlin (Prok.-Ost.), 247.
*Engr.* Rev. Num., N.S., vol. ix., Pl. I. 1.

Poseidon, to whom the horse was sacred, occurs on the Cyzicene staters, and it is probable that the horse may have been used as a coin-type in connection with him. It may, however, have been introduced as a copy of the coinage of Maronea, where it had been, in alliance with the vine, the long-continued badge of that city.

127. Pegasus flying to right. Beneath, tunny right.
    W. G. (*a*), 247·1 grs. (Bompois sale, No. 1363) [Pl. V. 21]. Brit. Mus. (*a*), 247·7. Paris (*b*), 246·9.
        (*a*) (*b*), diff. dies.
    *Engr.* Num. Chron., N.S., xvi., Pl. VIII. 23.

A type connected with the myth of Bellerophon; another type, the chimæra (Nos. 119, 120) equally belonging to the same legend, has already been described. The stater may have been copied from the long-continued and widely diffused coins of Corinth and her colonies, with which state Cyzicus, in its commercial relations, must necessarily have been in frequent contact. The worship of the Lycian hero had, however, at an early period spread into the neighbourhood of Cyzicus, which was, moreover, in many ways connected with Lycia, and we may perhaps regard the type as of local origin.

128. Forepart of winged horse to left. Beneath, tunny left.
    Brit. Mus., 40·9 grs. [Pl. V. 22]. Paris (De L.)
        Diff. dies.
    *Engr.* Sestini, Stat. Ant., Pl. VI. 14.
    *Noted.* Num. Vet. R. P. K., p. 138. Mionnet, Suppl., v. p. 369, No. 548.
    Twelfth. Brit. Mus., 19·2 grs.

The forepart of a winged horse was the badge or arms of the adjacent city of Lampsacus, and it occurs on the coinage of other towns of the district. It would, therefore, be strange if it was not found on the currency of so important a neighbouring state as Cyzicus.

It has, however, been suggested to me by Professor Gardner that the animal is not a horse but a deer or antelope, and he thinks he sees some indication of horns. It is certainly not a good representation of a horse, and has more of the form of the deer, both in the slenderness of the neck and the length of the head. If a stater of the same type should come to light the difficulty might be solved.

129. Ass standing left on tunny.
W. G., 246·2 grs. (Whittall sale, 1884, No. 757), [Pl. V. 23].

A Dionysiac type. It occurs upon many of the coins of Mende.

130. Ram standing to left on tunny.
W. G. (*a*), 247·5 grs. [Pl. V. 24]. Brit. Mus. (*b*), 247·4. Weber (*b*), 247. (Subhi sale, No. 1149.) Lambros (*b*).
(*a*), (*b*), diff. dies.
*Engr.* Num. Chron., N.S., xvi. Pl. VIII. 30.
*Noted.* Brandis, p. 404.
Hecta. Paris (De L.), 41·3 grs.
*Engr.* Sestini, Stat. Ant., Pl. VIII. 4.
*Noted.* Brandis, p. 404.

The ram, which occurs on others of the staters, may have found a place there in connection with the myth of Helle. On a gold stater of the neighbouring state of Lampsacus Helle is represented riding on the ram. The Argonautic expedition is so intimately connected with the history of Cyzicus that we may expect to find incidents of the story recorded on the Cyzicene coinage. The sacrifice of the ram by Phrixus to Zeus Phyxius, and the subsequent presentation of its golden fleece to Aeetes, may be considered the starting point of the expedition.

It is, perhaps, scarcely to be expected that the ram should occur on the coinage of maritime Cyzicus as a symbol of Apollo, the shepherd god (καρνεῖος), though in other relations he is frequent on the Cyzicenes.

131. Ram, with head turned back, kneeling left on tunny.
> Brit. Mus., 247·6 grs. [Pl. V. 25]. W. G., 249. Lambros in 1885.
> > All the same die.
>
> *Engr.* Sestini, Stat. Ant., Pl. VIII. 5. Brit. Mus. Guide, Pl. X. 9.
>
> *Noted.* Num. Vet., R. P. K., p. 117.

132. Forepart of ram running to left. Behind, tunny upwards.
> W. G., 248·3 grs. [Pl. V. 26]. Weber, 249·2.
> > Both the same die.

133. Goat kneeling left on tunny.
> Copenhagen 247 grs. (Ivanoff sale, No. 191.), [Pl. V. 27]. W. G. 246·3.
> > Diff. dies.
>
> *Noted.* Brandis, p. 404.
>
> Hecta. Berlin (Prok.-Ost.), 41·3 grs. [Pl. V. 28].

It is probably in connection with Dionysus that the goat occurs on the Cyzicene coins, though it may have been placed there as sacred to Hermes.

134. Head of goat to left. Behind, tunny upwards.
> Bunbury (*a*), 247 grs. (Dupré sale). [Pl. V. 29]. Brit. Mus. (*b*), 247·6. Paris (De L.), 249. St. Pet., 247. W. G. (*c*), 247·5. (Bompois sale, No. 1361). Lewis, 248·6. Löbbecke (*d*), 249·5. Hoffmann (two), 247, 247·2. Lambros in 1885 (two).
> > (*a*), (*b*), (*c*), (*d*), diff. dies.

*Engr.* Mionnet, Suppl., v., Pl. II. 1. Num. Chron., N.S., xvii., Pl. VI. 11.

*Noted.* Num. Vet., R. P. K., p. 106. Brandis, p. 404.

Hecta. Berlin (Fox), 41·4 grs. Six, 41·7, (Ivanoff sale, No. 154.)

Twelfth. Brit. Mus., 19·9 grs. Paris, 20·1.

*Noted.* Brandis, p. 404.

135. Boar walking left on tunny.
Vienna, 246 grs. [Pl. V. 30]. St. Pet., 247. Both same die.

Hecta. Imhoof (*a*), 41 grs. [Pl. V. 31]. Paris (De L.) (*b*), 40·8. Berlin, 41.3. W. G. (*b*), 39·7. (*a*), (*b*), diff. dies.

*Noted.* Brandis, p. 391, under Methymna.

The boar occurs on the early coins of Methymna.

136. Sow walking left on tunny.
Munich, 248·8 grs. [Pl. V. 32].

*Engr.* Sestini, Stat. Ant., Pl. IV. 27.

*Noted.* Mionnet, Suppl. v., p. 304, No. 125. Brandis, p. 391, under Methymna, and he calls the animal a boar.

Hecta. Brit. Mus. (*a*), 41 grs. Paris (*a*), 41·6. Hunter. Leake.

(*a*) same die.

*Engr.* Hunter, Pl. LXVI. 2. Sestini, Stat. Ant., Pl. IV. 28. Brit. Mus. Guide, Pl. X. 15.

*Noted.* Mionnet, vi., p. 615, No. 14. Suppl. v., p. 304, No. 126. Suppl. ix., p. 231, No. 27. Leake, Num. Hellen. Asiat. Greece, p. 50. Brandis, p. 405.

Twelfth. Waddington, 20·2 grs.

The sow is found on one of the early unattributed staters of the Phœnician standard, which have on the reverse a square incuse, divided into four parts by thin raised lines.

137. Forepart of winged boar swimming to left. Beneath, tunny left.
>Paris (*a*), 247·7 grs. [Pl. V. 33]. Brit. Mus. (*b*), 247·8. (Subhi sale, No. 764). W. G. (*b*), 247·6.
>>(*a*), (*b*), diff. dies.
>*Engr.* Mionnet, Suppl. v., Pl. II. 2.

The distinctive type of many silver coins attributed to Clazomenæ. It is found on an early electrum stater of the Phœnician standard, also attributed to Clazomenæ, of which this stater may be a copy.

138. Dog standing left on tunny, right fore-paw raised.
>Paris, 188·7 grs.[46]  [Pl. V. 34]. St. Pet., 237.
>>Diff. dies.
>*Engr.* Sestini, Stat. Ant., Pl. VIII. 13. Mionnet, Pl. XLIII. 2.
>*Noted.* Mionnet, iii., p. 176, No. 816. Brandis, p. 403.
>Hecta. Brit. Mus. (two) 41·2 grs., 40·6. [Pl. V. 35]. Paris, 40·1. Berlin (three) Fox, 40 ; Prok.-Ost. (two) 42·8, 41·5. Copenhagen. St. Pet. W. G., 41·8. Six (two), 42·3, 41 (Subhi sale, No. 767).
>*Noted.* Brandis, p. 403.
>Twelfth. Paris. Six, 20·8 grs.
>>Diff. dies.
>*Engr.* Sestini, Stat. Ant., Pl. IV. 17.
>*Noted.* Mionnet, Suppl. v., p. 302, No. 114.

In the Allier de Hauteroche Collection (Pl. XIV. 12) was a silver coin, attributed to Colophon, precisely like the stater. It has on the reverse a quadripartite square incuse. It is engraved Sestini, Stat. Ant., Pl. VIII. 15. This, possibly, may be an instance where Cyzicus, as in other

---

[46] The weight is much below the standard, and the coin is probably plated.

cases, adopted the type of another state; here the town was Colophon.

139. Forepart of dog to left, head turned back. Behind, tunny upwards.

Imhoof (*a*), 34 grs. [Pl. V. 36]. Munich, 41·3. Six (*b*), 41·3 (Ivanoff sale, No. 155).
(*a*), (*b*), diff. dies.

*Engr.* Sestini, Stat. Ant., Pl. VIII. 14.

140. Winged dog, crouching to left on tunny, head turned back.

W. G., 249·3 grs. [Pl. VI. 1].

Hecta. Munich (*a*), 41·9 grs. [Pl. VI. 2]. Paris (*b*), 41·8. Berlin (plated), 28·8. Waddington, 39·7.
(*a*), (*b*), diff. dies.

*Engr.* Sestini, Stat. Ant., Pl. IX. 4.

141. Cerberus standing to left. He has two heads with a collar round each neck, and the tail ends in the head of a serpent. Beneath, tunny left.

Brit. Mus. (*a*), 250·4 grs. [Pl. VI. 3]. W. G. (*b*), 246·8. One sold by Sotheby and Wilkinson, Feb. 19, 1887, 250·4 grs. A second sold by S. & W., Mar. 22, 1887, 240 grs.
(*a*), (*b*), diff. dies.

*Engr.* Num. Chron., N.S., vol. xvi., Pl. VIII. 24.

Hecta. Paris, 41 grs. St. Pet. (*a*), 42·4. Six (*a*), 40·8. (Hamilton sale, 1867).
(*a*) same die.

*Noted.* Brandis, p. 404.

Cerberus, as overpowered and chained, when Theseus was delivered from Hades, forms an incident in the myth of Heracles, with which several of the types on the Cyzicene coins are connected. Mr. Head (Num. Chron., N.S., xvi. p. 284) suggests that the type was derived from

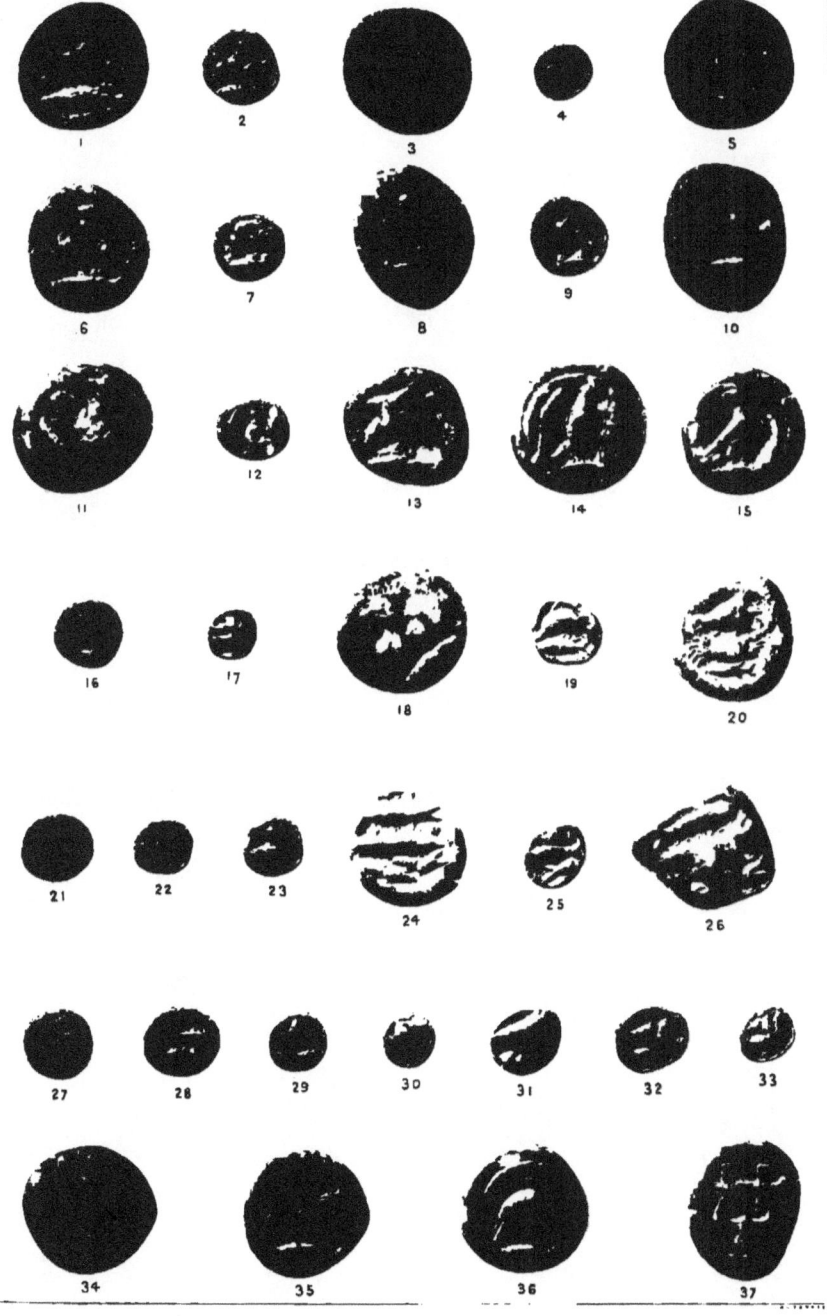

Cimmerium, anciently called Cerberion, with which district Cyzicus was in constant commercial intercourse.

142. Animal with long tail standing to left on tunny.
Twelfth. Brit. Mus., 20·7 grs. [Pl. VI. 4].
*Noted.* Num. Vet., R. P. K., p. 3.

The animal, which has much the appearance of a squirrel, is no doubt a fox, and was placed on the coin in connection with Bassareus, the Lydian Dionysus, to whom the animal was sacred. On the reverses of early electrum staters and half-staters attributed to Miletus and to Lydia (Head, Hist. Num. pp. 503, 545), there is a figure of a running fox within an oblong incuse, between two small incuse squares containing respectively a stag's head and a cross with pellets at the extremities.

143. Griffin, with rounded wings, standing left on tunny, the right fore-paw raised.
W. G. (*a*), 247·2 grs. [Pl. VI. 5]. Brit. Mus. (*a*), 245·2. Paris (De L.) (*b*), 247·8. Hague (*b*), 247·4. Waddington (Northwick sale, No. 956). Weber, 244·2 (Whittall sale, 1884, No. 750). Löbbecke, 246·9. Lambros.
(*a*), (*b*), diff. dies.
*Engr.* Sestini, Stat. Ant., Pl. IX. 1. Num. Chron., N.S., xvi., Pl. VIII. 25.
*Noted.* Num. Vet., R. P. K., p. 154. Brandis, p. 398, under Teos.
Hecta. Berlin, 40·1 grs.

There is no type, except the lion, which occurs so frequently on the staters as the griffin. And in connection with Apollo, the father of its mythical founder, we might expect it to be common. As the guardian of the gold in the land of the Hyperboreans, periodically visited by Apollo, the griffin might again find a place on the Cyzicene coinage, and with more than ordinary fitness, as the gold used at Cyzicus came principally, through Panticapæum, from the region where the Hyperboreans were supposed to dwell. The griffin, as the common type, the badge of Teos and Abdera, its colony, both of them not far distant and wealthy states, was also to be expected on the coins of a city which so frequently adopted the monetary subjects of other states. Though, probably, used on the coinage of Cyzicus in connection with Apollo, the griffin was also a Dionysiac symbol. Types having reference to Dionysus and his worship are very common on the staters, and it is evident that he was held in especial reverence in Cyzicus.

144. Griffin, with rounded wing, seated to left on tunny, the right fore-paw raised.
Brit. Mus., 248·8 grs. [Pl. VI. 6]. W. G., 247·1, (Subhi sale, No. 766). Lambros in 1885.
All the same die.
*Engr.* Num. Chron., N.S., vol. xvii., Pl. VI. 8.

145. Griffin, with pointed wing, standing to left on tunny, the right fore-paw raised.
Berlin, 89·7 grs. [Pl. VI. 7].

146. Griffin, with pointed wing, seated left on tunny.
Brit. Mus., 247·5 grs. [Pl. VI. 8].
*Engr.* Num. Chron., N.S., xvii., Pl. VI. 9.
Hecta. Munich, 39·6 grs. [Pl. VI. 9].
*Engr.* Sestini, Stat. Ant., Pl. IX. 2.

147. Griffin to left on tunny, holding head of spear in mouth.
Mionnet, Suppl. v., p. 202, No. 112, (Cab. de feu M. d'Hermand).

I have been unable to trace this coin, and I think it probable that it is wrongly described. It is the common type on coins of Panticapæum, and one which might be expected to occur on the coinage of Cyzicus, supposing that the coin as described ever existed.

148. Forepart of griffin to left, with rounded wing. Beneath, tunny left.

W. G. (*a*), 246·6 grs. [Pl. VI. 10]. Hoffmann (two), (*b*), 246·8.

(*a*), (*b*), diff. dies.

Hecta. Munich, 41 grs.

*Engr.* Sestini, Stat. Ant., Pl. IX. 3.

*Noted.* Mionnet, vi., p. 616, No. 26.

Twelfth. St. Pet., 18·7 grs.

*Noted.* Mionnet, vi., p. 616, No. 27.

The griffin on this stater is represented with the head of a lion; on all the others the head is the ordinary one of an eagle or kindred bird.

149. Forepart of griffin to left, with rounded wings. In front, tunny upwards.

Brit. Mus., 250 grs. (Subhi sale, No. 209). [Pl. VI. 11].

150. Griffin's head and neck to left, on each side a tunny upwards.

Six, 41·8 grs. (Gréau sale, No. 1652). [Pl. VI. 12].

151. Eagle, with wings raised, to left on tunny and apparently about to tear it.

W. G., 246·1 grs. [Pl. VI. 13].

A type very similar, except that the hare, &c., is replaced by the tunny, to one frequent on the coins of

Elis. An eagle standing on a dolphin is the ordinary type of Sinope.

152. Eagle facing, but flying to right, behind, tunny downwards, all upon disk or within a circle.
Paris, 247 grs. [Pl. VI. 14]. Berlin, 246·9.
Diff. dies.
*Engr.* Rev. Num., N.S., ix., Pl. I. 6.

The disk probably represents the sun, and if so the type is connected with Helios, the sun-god.

153. Eagle, with head turned back, standing to right on tunny, all upon disk.
Berlin, 247·9 grs. [Pl. VI. 15].
*Engr.* Rev. Num., N.S., ix., Pl. I. 2.

154. Eagle standing to right upon tunny; above it is a second tunny whose head is covered by that of the eagle.
Six, 40·8 grs. (Subhi sale, No. 767). [Pl. VI. 16].
Twelfth. W. G., 20·8 grs. [Pl. VI. 17]. Kotschoubey Coll., 20·2.
*Engr.* De Koehne, Mus. Kotschoubey, Pl. I. 1.

155. Forepart of cock, with rounded wing, to left. Beneath, tunny left.
Brit. Mus., 248·2 grs. (Subhi sale, No. 765). [Pl. VI. 18].

The bird commonly offered in sacrifice to Asclepios was a cock, and the type may have reference to the worship of that god, whose head occurs on hectæ of Phocæa. The cock as the bird of dawn is the common type of Himera, but it does not appear probable that there is any copying here of the Sicilian coin. On the coins of Dardanus in Troas the cock is of frequent occurrence, though commonly it is a fighting cock. It is found, however, in a peaceful attitude upon an early electrum stater of the Phœnician standard, as well as upon silver coins of a little later date.

156. Head of fish, with spike, to left. Beneath, head of cock turned towards the fish-head.

Imhoof, 42 grs.

This hecta, one of the class with the fish-head, probably representing the whole tunny, came into Dr. Imhoof-Blumer's collection too late to be included in the plates. It was sent to him from Trebizond.

157. Dolphin to left. Beneath, tunny left.
Brit. Mus. (two), 41·6 grs., 40·4. [Pl. VI. 19].
Diff. dies.
*Noted.* Num. Vet., R. P. K., p. 141.
Twelfth. Brit. Mus. (two), 20·7 grs. (*a*), 20·5 (*b*). W. G. (*a*), 20·8.
(*a*), (*b*), diff. dies.

A type connected with Poseidon, who on the stater, No. 6, holds a dolphin on his hand.

158. Crab holding in its claws the head of a fish to left. Beneath, small tunny left.
Imhoof, 248·7 grs. [Pl. VI. 20].
*Noted.* Imhoof-Blumer, Monn. Grecq., p. 242, No. 78.
Hecta. Brit. Mus., 86 grs. [Pl. VI. 21].
Of base gold. There is no tunny beneath the crab.

A type, like the last, probably connected with the worship of Poseidon. Upon the stater No. 161 the claws only of a crab are represented, together with two fish. Dr. Imhoof-Blumer believes the fish not to be a tunny, and that the fabric of the coin differs in some degree from that of the Cyzicene staters. For these reasons, and also because on the corresponding hecta the fish is absent, he thinks the coin belongs to another state than Cyzicus. He suggests that what appears to be the head of a fish held by the crab is a sun-fish. It is quite true that the fabric of this stater and of No. 161, as well as of the corresponding hectæ and twelfths, which have upon them the head or tail of a fish and other like devices, is different from that of the ordinary Cyzicenes. The fish on these archaic coins differs also from the usual representation of the tunny of Cyzicus. The monetary system is, however, the same, and the incuse of the reverse is of essentially the same form as that of the acknowledged coins of Cyzicus, while the fish may well be the tunny, though not executed with the same truth to nature. I have, therefore, included this most peculiar and puzzling class of coins (Nos. 158, 161 to 168) among the electrum series of Cyzicus, though with a little hesitation.

159. Crab. Beneath, tunny right.
    Hoffmann in 1879, 14·8 grs. [Pl. VI. 22].

I have not been able to trace this coin, of which M. Six has kindly given me a cast, taken from it when in M. Hoffmann's possession.

160. Pecten shell, hinge downwards. Beneath, tunny left.
    Brit. Mus., 21·1 grs. [Pl. VI. 23].
    *Engr.* Sestini, Stat. Ant., Pl. VI. 20.
    *Noted.* Num. Vet., R. P. K., p. 150.

161. Two fish to left, with a dot between their tails. Beneath, two crab claws.

   Imhoof, 249·5 grs. [Pl. VI. 24]. Berlin, 249·8.

   *Engr.* Rev. de la Numis. Belge, vol. v., p. 248, Pl. VII. 1.

162. Tunny to left, above head of fish, with spike projecting from it behind, to right. Beneath, tail of fish to right.

   Imhoof, 41·8 grs. [Pl. VI. 25]. Lambros, 28·1 (plated).

163. Head of fish with spike, to left, behind a trifid fleur-de-lys-shaped object (a flower ?). Above, tunny right.

   Imhoof, 250 grs. [Pl. VI. 26].

   Hecta. Brit. Mus., 41·5 grs. [Pl. VI. 27]. Leake, 41·3.

   *Noted.* Leake, Num. Hellen. Suppl., p. 44.

The hecta has no trifid object, but only the spike, with a dot above it.

164. Head of fish, with spike, to right. Above, tunny to right, over whose tail is a trifid flower (?) upright.

   Paris, 42 grs. [Pl. VI. 28].

165. Head of fish, with spike, to right. Beneath, tunny right.

   Paris, 20·8 grs. [Pl. VI. 29]. W. G., 20·6.
   Diff. dies.

166. Head of fish, with spike, to right. Above it tunny (?). Beneath, tunny left.

   Paris, 21·6 grs. [Pl. VI. 30].

167. Head of fish, with spike, to left. Beneath, tail of fish to left.

   Paris, 41·8 grs. [Pl. VI. 31].

168. Two fish-heads, each with spike, to left, one above the other. Behind them tunny upwards. In field to right two dots; and in field to left one dot.
Hirsch, 41·7 grs. [Pl. VI. 32].
Twelfth. Brit. Mus., 14·3 grs. [Pl. VI. 33].
*Noted.* Num. Vet., R. P. K., p. 150.

The twelfth is of very pale electrum, and has two dots, one above and the other beneath the fish-heads.

169. Pistrix to right. Beneath, tunny right.
W. G., 248·2 grs. [Pl. VI. 34].

A type probably connected with Poseidon, if it is anything more than a copy of a portion of another coin. The pistrix is found in the exergue, beneath the chariot, upon a large series of the earlier tetradrachms, &c., of Syracuse. Mr. Head has suggested, with much probability, that it was placed there to commemorate the naval victory gained by Hieron over the Etruscans near Cumæ, B.C. 474.

Upon a vase where Poseidon is represented as crushing Ephialtes with a rock, among other creatures of the sea, is a pistrix.[47]

170. Prow of a ship to left, from which issues the forepart of a winged wolf. Beneath, tunny left.
Paris (De L.), 248 grs. [Pl. VI. 35]. Imhoof, 249·2. Both the same die.
*Engr.* Rev. Num., N.S., vol. i., Pl. II. 6. Mon. Ined. dell' Inst. Archeol., vol. iii., Pl. XXXV. 20.

The expedition of the Argonauts plays an important part in the mythical history of Cyzicus, and the prow

---

[47] Lenormant and De Witte, Élite des Mon. Céram, vol. i., Pl. V.

represented on the stater is probably that of the ship Argo. The ordinary type on the coinage of Cius in Bithynia is a prow, and that place is also connected with the Argonautic myth.

171. Crested Corinthian helmet to left. Beneath, tunny left.
    Imhoof, 248·6 grs. [Pl. VI. 36].
    *Noted.* Imhoof-Blumer, Monn. Grecq., p. 242. No. 72.

Though the helmet is of Corinthian, and not Athenian form, it may possibly be in connection with Pallas that it is placed on the stater.

172. Lyre. Beneath, tunny right.
    Paris (De L.) (*a*), 246·1 grs. [Pl. VI. 37]. Paris, 245·8.
        Imhoof (*a*), 246·2.
            (*a*) same die.
    *Engr.* Mionnet, Suppl. v., Pl. III. 1.
    *Noted.* Brandis, p. 409.
    Twelfth. Paris, 19·5 grs.
    *Noted.* Brandis, p. 409.

A type connected with Apollo makes a fitting termination to the long and varied series of the electrum coins of Cyzicus.

# INDEX.

## A.

Abdera, Heracles seated on coin of, 85; large variety of coin-types, 21
Abydus, coins of, 13
Achelöus, defeat of, by Heracles, 85
Actæon, head of, 24, 60; represented on vases, 60
Ægospotami, battle of, 6, 19, 76
Æsepus, the river, possibly represented on stater, 73, 74
Agalmata, primitive, 5
Agrigentum, head of eagle and crab claw on coin of, 61
Alexander the Great, his staters found with Cyzicenes, 42
Alliance, states in, after battle of Cnidus, 83
Androcydes, a Cyzicene painter, 73
Antalcidas, peace of, 7
Aphrodite, 25; head of, 65; with Eros, 66
Apollo, 5, 10, 24; destroyer of Python, 55; head of, 54, 55; holding lyre, 56, 57; Hyperborean, 11, 56; seated on griffin, 56, 57; seated on swan, 57; shooting, 55; wearing ear-ring, 91; worshipped as Lycius, 10
Aradus, Dagon on coin of, 51
Argo, the ship, 26, 125
Argonauts, 5, 12, 124; figure of one, 96, 99
Art at Cyzicus, 35; of staters the only test of date, 31, 34; rapid development of, 75
Artemis, 10, 11, 24; harbour-guardian, 11; her worship brought from Miletus, 11
Asclepius, 25
Asiatic standard, early electrum coins of, 14, 15, 29
Ass, 112
Astacus, coins of, 45
Athena plants olive-trees at Athens, 65; treasury of, in the Parthenon, 14
Athens, coinage of, 8; defeated at Chios, 7; her commercial interests in the Euxine, 19; long connected with Cyzicus, 28, 61; types connected with, 28, 37, 61; uniformity of her coin-type, 8, 40
Atys, 9, 25; head of, 78, 79

## B.

Bassareus, the Lydian Dionysus, 25; fox the symbol of, 117
Bellerophon, 26; myth of, 108, 111
Berlin, terracotta there with Gaia and Cecrops, 63
Bifrontal head, 72
Boar, 114; forepart of winged, 115
Briareus, one of the giants, 5
Bull, 109; butting, 109; forepart of winged, 110; head of, 110; human-headed, 73; walking, 109

## C.

Cabeirus, head of a, 86
Camarina, figure on swan on coins of, 57
Cecrops, 25, 64, 65; represented on vases, 65
Centaur, 71
Cerberus, 26, 116
Chabrias, statue of, 98
Cheiron, Jason brought up by, 71
Chimæra, 108
Chios, coin-type of, 101; defeat of Athens at, 7

Cimmerium, anciently Cerberion, 117
Classification of staters in regard to date, 32, 33
Clazomenæ, hoard of staters found near, 41; coin-type of, 115
Cleite, daughter of Merops, wife of Cyzicus, 4, 5
Cnidus, battle off, 6, 76
Cock, forepart of, 120; head of, 121
Coin-types, see Types
Coin-weight of Cyzicus, 14 n, 23
Coinage authenticated by the badge of the State, 8
Coins circulate long after they cease to be issued, 34
Conon, his victory off Cnidus, 6, 76
Cora, head of, on coins of Cyzicus, 52
Corinth, coin-type of, 111
Cow, a black, sacrificed to Persephone, 11
Crab, 121, 122; claws of, 123
Cray-fish, on reverse of stater, 45
Crœsus, gold coinage of, 45
Critios, group in marble by, 90
Cumæ, Scylla on coins of, 73
Currency, no gold or silver in early times at Cyzicus, 13
CURTIUS, Dr. Ernst, on religious character of coin-types, 7
Cybele, 9, 10, 25, 78; chryselephantine statue of, 78; feast in honour of, 10; seated on lion, 77, 78; worship of, in Mysia, 78
Cynossema, battle of, 6
Cypselus, chest of, representation of Fear on, 80; of Gorgons pursuing Perseus, 89
Cyrenaica, silphium the badge of, 46
Cyrus overthrows Lydian empire, 6
Cyzicus (the hero), 26; head of, 92; reputed founder of the city, 12; slain by Jason or Heracles, 5; son of Apollo, 4; tomb at Cyzicus, 12
Cyzicus (the city), badge of, 22; battle of, 6, 72, 75; beauty of its buildings, 9; celebrated for its wine, 70; earliest settlers there, 3; eclectic character of coin-types, 36; founded by colony from Miletus, 5; given to Persephone by Zeus, 11; its importance as a trading community, 12; no gold or silver currency, 13; position of, 3; protected by Persephone, 12; religious cults prevailing there, 8; scene of rape of Persephone, 12, 53; school of painting there, 35, 36; siege of, by Mithradates, 11; site of, not excavated, 36; tribes into which it was divided, 5; tunny the badge of, 22, 45; under Athenian influence, 6, 7; under Persian rule, 6, 7; under Sparta, 6; used types foreign to herself, 27; wealth of, 13

D.

Dagon, on coins of Aradus, 51
Dardanus, coins of, 120
Darics, 14, 16, 17; current with Cyzicenes, 35; found with Cyzicenes, 41
Delphi, omphalos of Apollo at, 58
Demeter, 12, 24, 52, 53; carried in serpent car, 54; head of, 51, 52; pursuing Hades, 54
Demetrius Poliorcetes, tetradrachm of with Nike, 75
Demosthenes, his account of the value of Cyzicene staters, 17; staters of Cyzicus current in his time, 34
Denominations of electrum coins, 13, 14; table of, 43, 44
Die-engravers, excellence of Cyzicene, 40; their skill in adapting subjects to space, 37
Die-engraving, not a true test of art, 35
Dindymene, name of Cybele, 9, 78
Dindymus, mountain in Phrygia, 9; mountain near Cyzicus, 5
Dionysiac subjects, novel treatment of, by Cyzicene artists, 38
Dionysus, 25, 67, 68; as a child, 68; head of, 66, 67; head of, on coins of Naxus and Thasus, 67; head of, on coins of Timotheus of Heraclea, 93; popular god at Cyzicus, 38; seated on rock covered with panther's skin, 67, 68; statue of, in form of a bull, 12, 109; youthful, 68
Discobolus, head of, 91
Divinities worshipped at Cyzicus, 9, seq.
Dog, 115; forepart of, 116; winged, 116
Doliones, settled at Cyzicus, 3
Dolphin, 48, 121
Double-stater of Cyzicus, 14

## E.

Eagle on disk, 120; on tunny, 119, 120
Eagles of Zeus at Delphi, 58, 59
ECKHEL, ignorant of existence of staters, 2, 18
Electrum, 14; artificial, 15, 16; harder than gold, 16; native, 15, 16
Electrum coins, denominations of, 13, 14; early issue of, 14, 18; had a special value, 17; not current as gold coin, 16
Electrum staters of Cyzicus, called gold staters, 17
Eleuthɛria, 76
Ephesus, early electrum coins of, 15
Erichthonius, 25, 37, 61, 63, 64, 65
Eros, 66; of Asiatic type, 82
Eupolis, his remark on the abundance of staters at Cyzicus, 19
Euxine, trade of Cyzicus with the, 12, 18, 19

## F.

Fear (Φόβος), figure of, 80
Fish-head, coins with, 121, 122, 123, 124
Fish-tail, figure with, 50; figure with, on coins of Itanus, 51
Fox, sacred to Bassareus, 25, 117
Friezes of temples supplied subjects for coin-types, 39

## G.

Gaia, 25, 37, 61, 63, 64; representation of, with Erichthonius and Cecrops, on terracotta, 63
Gela, coin-type of, 26, 28, 37, 74
Goat, 25, 113; head of, 113
Gods, types connected with, on staters, 23
Gold, analysis of Siberian, 20; found in Asia Minor, 19; from Ural Mountains, 13, 16, 19, 20, 56; guarded by griffins, 11, 56, 118; supply of, for staters, 19; value of, at Panticapæum, 20; value of, in Greece, 20; well known in Greece, 16
Gorgon-head, 25, 63, 89
Gorgons pursuing Perseus, 89
Granicus, battle at, 77
Greece, value of gold there in proportion to silver, 20
Griffin, 117, 118; forepart of, 119; head of, 119
Griffins guarding gold, 11, 56, 118
Gyges, King of Lydia, 6

## H.

Hades, helmet of, lent to Perseus, 88
Harmodius and Aristogeiton, 25, 37, 90
Harpa of Perseus, 105
Harpy, 100; forepart of, 100
Head on a disk, 90
HEAD, Mr. Barclay V., account of a hoard of staters, 2; his opinion on the annual issue of types, 30
Hectæ of Phocæa, &c., 18
Helios, 24, 59; head of, 91; worshipped at Zeleia, 59
Helle, myth of, 112
Hellenic coinage, religious character of, 7
Hellenic race, its spirit of commercial enterprise, 3
Hellenic State, its polity inseparable from its religion, 7
Helmet, 125; held by figure in the hand, 96; terminating in wing, 88, 89
Helmeted figure, 96, 98, 99
Hera instigates giants to kill Heracles, 5; serpents sent by, to destroy Heracles, 83
Heracles, 26; and Iphicles, 83; called Founder on a coin of Cyzicus, 83; head of, 82; holding club over head, 84, 85; holding horn, 85; seated, 85; strangling Nemean lion, 86; strangling serpents, 64, 83; with the Argonauts, 5, 12, 82; youthful, 96
Hermes, 25; goat connected with, 25; head of, 25, 66
Hoards of staters, 41, 42
HOFMANN, Dr. K. B., specific gravity of staters, 14, 15
Hoplite, preparing for, or winning in, the race, 97
Horse, 110; winged, 111
Human-headed bull, 73

## I.

IMHOOF-BLUMER, Dr., doubts if fish is the tunny, 122; regards lion-headed man as a figure of Fear, 80; thinks head of a fish is a sunfish, 122
Incuse, of first issue of Cyzicene stater, 21; on reverse of coin, retained throughout on the staters, 22
Inscription, found only on a single stater, 22

Itanus, figure with fish-tail ou coin of, 51

### J.
Jason, 5, 26, 99

### K.
Kertch, staters found near, 20, 41
KOFHNE, DE, account of stater with Apollo on swan, 58 ; with Nereid, 72

### L.
Lampsacus, coins of, 13. 16 ; stater of, with Nereid, 72; staters of, found with Cyzicenes, 41; winged horse, badge of, 111
Larissa, daughter of Piasus, 4
LENORMANT, M. Charles, Essai sur les Statères de Cyzique, 2 ; his belief that the Cyzicenes belong principally to the fourth century, 19 ; his opinion of date of stater with Nike holding an aplustre, 75 ; his untenable theory about date of stater with Eleutheria, 77
LENORMANT, M. François, believes the principal issue of staters was after B.C. 404, 33, 34 ; Statères inédits de Cyzique, 2 ; subject on stater attributed by him to Phrixus sacrificing ram with golden fleece, 87
Lion, 102, 103, 104, 105 ; biting harpa, 105 ; connected with Cybele, 103 ; forepart of, 106 ; head of, 107 ; scalp of, 106 ; sun symbol, 103
Lion-headed man, 79, 80
Lioness, 104 ; forepart of, 105, 106 ; head of, 107 ; winged, 107
Lycius, Apollo as, worshipped at Zeleia, 10
Lydia, early coinage of, 15 ; gold coinage of, 31, 45 ; kingdom of, 6
Lyre, 125 ; Apollo holding, 56

### M.
Macedon, gold mines of, 19
Magisterial devices, principal subject on the Cyzicenes, 30 ; elsewhere subordinate to badge of state, 30
Magistrates, marks on coins designating, 29
Mallus, winged figure on coins of, 81
Maronea, coin-type of, 110
MARQUARDT, Cyzicus und sein Gebiet, 2

Medusa, head of, carried by Perseus, 89
Megara, colony from, to Cyzicus, 6
Merops, King of Percote, 4
Miletus, Cyzicus founded by colony from, 5 ; electrum coinage of, 15 ; temple of Apollo there, 10
MILLINGEN, his theory of date of stater with Eleutheria, 77
Mill-sail pattern on reverse of staters, 22
Mithradates besieges Cyzicus, 11
Monasteries in Middle Ages possessed of much wealth, 7
Monetary value of staters, 17
Mortal, early representation of, on coin, 90
Munychia, temple of Artemis there, 11

### N.
Name of city not found on the Cyzicenes, 22
Naxus, head of Dionysus on coins of, 67
Nereid seated on dolphin, 72
Nike, 26 ; flying, 76 ; goddess of agonistic victory, 75 ; goddess of victory in war, 75 ; holding aplustre. 74
Niobe and her children on coin of Erchomenus in Arcadia, 55

### O.
Odysseus, 26 ; head of, 86 ; slaying ram, 87
Olive-tree planted by Athena, 65
Olympian hierarchy, gods of 23
Omphalos of Apollo at Delphi, 58
Orestes at Delphi, 26, 87 ; represented on vases, 88
Oriental character of coin-type, 79
Oriental cults, types of, 27

### P.
Pactolus, gold from the river, 15
Painting, school of, at Cyzicus, 35, 36
Pallas, head of, 24, 60, 61, 62
Pan, head of, 28, 69
Panticapœum, 12, 19, 20 ; value of silver there, 20 ; weight of gold stater there, 20
Pecten shell, 122
Pegasus, 111
Pelasgi settled at Cyzicus, 4

Pergamon, frieze there with Cybele on lion, 78; with lion-headed man, 80
Persephone, black cow sacrificed to, 11; carried off by Hades, 54; changes rocks into the island Bespicus, 5; Cyzicus given by Zeus to, 11; Cyzicus protected by, 12; Cyzicus the scene of the rape of, 12, 53; worshipped at Cyzicus, 11
Perseus carrying head of Medusa, 89; harpa of, 105; head of, 26, 88; pursued by Gorgons, 89
Persian king, head of, 93
Persian power in Asia Minor broken, 77
Persian rule, Cyzicus under, 6
Perspective, inability to represent objects in, 63
Pharnabazus, daric struck during satrapy of, 13n; Peisander defeated by, at Cnidus, 6; proclaims autonomy to Greek cities of Asia Minor, 76
Philip of Macedon, his gold staters, 18, 35
Phocæa, hectæ of, 17, 18, 22; type of, 29
Phocaic standard, in use at Cyzicus for electrum coinage, 13, 21, 45
Phrixus sacrificing ram with golden fleece, 87; statue of, at Athens, 87
Phrygians from Thrace settled at Cyzicus, 4
Piasus, a Thessalian king, 4
Piræus, hoard of staters found there, 35, 42
Pistrix, 124
Polydectes, Perseus bringing head of Medusa to, 89
Poseidon, 24; head of, 48; holding dolphin, 48, 49; striking with trident, 49
Poseidonia, coin-type of, 29
Prow of ship, 124

R.

Ram, 112. 113; forepart of, 113; Helle riding on, 112
Religious character of Hellenic coinage, 7
Reverse, nature of, on staters, 22
Rhea, 9
Rhea-Cybele, temple of, at Cyzicus, 5
Rhodian coins, head of Helios on, 91
River-god, 26, 73

Rose, M. C., analysis of Siberian gold, 20

S.

Same event commemorated on two coins, 75
Samos, coin-type of, 29
Satyr drinking from amphora, 70; holding flute, 71; holding tunny, 69; pouring wine into cantharus, 70
Satyric mask, 71
Scylla, 26, 73; picture of, by Androcydes, 73
Scythian warrior, 99
Sestini, Stateri Antichi, 2, *passim*
Sicyon, Apollo on coin of, 55, 56; coin-types of, 28
Silphium, badge of the Cyrenaica, 46
Silver, its value at Pantiсapæum, 20
Six, M., 2, 30, 34, 55
Sow, 114
Spata, early ivories found at, 100
Spartan rule in Asia overthrown, 76
Specific gravity of Cyzicene staters, 14, 15
Sphinx, 101, 102; forepart of, 102
Standard, the Phocaic, in use at Cyzicus, 13, 21, 45
Stater of Cyzicus, a double. 14; monetary value of, 17; one a month's pay of Xenophou's soldiers, 17
Staters of Cyzicus, classed with darics, 17; great trading medium, 18, 34; no analysis of, 14; not issued as gold coins, 16; specific gravity of, 14, 15; stored in treasuries, 17, 18; subjects on, 38, 39; time of their issue, 31, 32, 33; two coinages of, 21, 22, 31; types of, 21, 22
Staters of Philip of Macedon, 18, 35
Sun-fish, 122
Symbol of the state, a religious one, 8
Syracuse, coin-type of, on stater, 29, 94

T.

Taras, son of Poseidon, 24, 49, 50
Tarentum, coin-types of, 24, 28, 37, 49, 50
Temple decorations, source of coin subjects, 39

Temples, coins issued from, 7, 8; numerous at Cyzicus, 8; receptacles of property, 7
Terracotta at Berlin with Gaia, Erichthonius and Cecrops, 63
Thasus, head of Dionysus on coins of, 67
Thebes, promoter of resistance to Sparta, 84; type of Heracles and serpents originated there, 84
Thetis, 26, 72
Thrace, gold mines of, 19
Thurium, coin-type of, 29, 110
Timotheus, dynast of Heraclea, coin of, 93
Triptolemus in serpent car, 53, 54; on coins of Athens and Eleusis, 54
Triton, 50, 51
Tunny, badge of Cyzicus, 22, 45; product of sea near Cyzicus, 22, 45; sacred to Aphrodite-Astarte, 46
Type, part of, representing the whole, 61
Types (coin), classification of, 23; copied by Cyzicus from other states, 36; copied from single figures or groups, 39; foreign to Cyzicene cults used on staters, 27; illustrative of religious cults, 21; of Cyzicene staters, 21, 22; of religious origin, 7, 8; the cause of diversity of, on staters, 29; usually local, 36

Tyra, coins of, 52
Tyrrheni, possess the Cyziene Chersonese, 4

U.

Ural Mountains, gold of, 13, 16, 19, 20, 56

V.

Value, monetary, of staters, 17

W.

Wealth accumulated by monasteries, 8; of Cyzicus, 13
Wine, Cyzicus celebrated for, 70
Winged, boar, 115; bull, 110; dog, 116; female figure, 80; horse, 111; lioness, 107; male figure, 79, 82
WROTH, Mr., Catalogue of Cretan Coins, 51

X.

Xenophon, his account of the pay of a soldier of the Ten Thousand, 17

Z.

Zeleia. Apollo worshipped there as Lycius, 10; Chimæra on coin of, 108; electrum stater attributed to, 108
Zeus, 23, 46; golden eagles of, at Delphi, 58, 59
Zeus-Ammon, head of, 47, 48

www.ingramcontent.com/pod-product-compliance
Lightning Source LLC
Chambersburg PA
CBHW022127160426
43197CB00009B/1177